The Kingdom of Heaven on Earth

Keys to the Kingdom of God in the Gospel of Matthew

JEFF DOLES

The Kingdom of Heaven on Earth
© 2009 by Jeff Doles

Published by
WALKING BAREFOOT MINISTRIES
P.O. Box 1062, Seffner, FL 33583

ISBN 10: 0-9823536-0-X
ISBN 13: 978-0-9823536-0-8

Cover photo © Gino Santa Maria. Image from *www.BigStockPhoto.com*.
Cover design and book interior by *www.ChristianBookDesign.com*

For more resources on enjoying new life in Christ, living in faith and the power of the Holy Spirit, or to find out more about Jeff Doles, visit our websites:

www.WalkingBarefoot.com
www.TheFaithLog.com
www.JeffDoles.com

Contents

The Sermon of Heaven on Earth

The Nature of Heaven on Earth

Introduction:
The Gospel of Heaven on Earth

Repent, for the kingdom of heaven is now at hand. (Matthew 4:17)

God created us to enjoy Heaven on Earth with Him. That was His plan from the beginning. After He created heaven and earth and every living thing, He said,

> *"Let Us make man in Our image, according to Our likeness; let them have dominion over the fish of the sea, over the birds of the air, and over the cattle, over all the earth and over every creeping thing that creeps on the earth."*
>
> *So God created man in His own image; in the image of God He create him; male and female He created them. Then God blessed them, and God said to them, "Be fruitful and multiply; fill the earth and subdue it; have dominion over the fish of the sea, over the birds of the air, and over every living thing that moves on the earth." (Genesis 1:26-28)*

God created man in His image and according to His likeness—that is, to be like Him. Then He blessed man and gave him dominion over all the earth. In this capacity, man was to be fruitful and multiply, to fill the earth and subdue it. To subdue the earth means to bring it into line with the purposes of God. Man was created in the likeness of God to bring the earth into the likeness of heaven—the will of God being done on earth as it is in heaven.

There was a problem, of course, as every child in Sunday school learns: Adam sinned. He disobeyed God and in his rebellion disconnected from the life of God (Genesis 3). The ground was cursed because of him and Heaven on Earth was lost. But God had a plan to restore creation to His original purpose. Since it was lost because of the rebellion of one man, Adam, it would require the obedience of one man, Messiah (Christ), to restore it.

> *Therefore, as through one man's offense judgment came to all men, result-*
> *ing in condemnation, even so through one Man's righteous act the free*
> *gift came to all men, resulting in justification of life. For as by one man's*
> *disobedience many were made sinners, so also by one Man's obedience many*
> *will be made righteous. Moreover the law entered that the offense might*
> *abound. But where sin abounded, grace abounded much more, so that as*
> *sin reigned in death, even so grace might reign through righteousness to*
> *eternal life through Jesus Christ our Lord. (Romans 5:18-21)*

God created a lineage through which this Man would come. He chose Abraham and gave Him a promise:

> *I will make you a great nation;*
> *I will bless you*
> *And make your name great;*
> *And you shall be a blessing.*
> *I will bless those who bless you,*
> *And I will curse him who curses you;*
> *And in you all the families of the earth shall be blessed.*
> *(Genesis 12:2-3)*

God made covenant with Abraham and gave him a son, Isaac. God confirmed the covenant with Isaac, and then with Isaac's son,

Jacob. God gave Jacob twelve sons. Jacob blessed them and, over one in particular, prophesied a king: "The scepter shall not depart from Judah, nor a lawgiver from between his feet, until Shiloh comes; and to Him shall be the obedience of the people" (Genesis 49:10). To Judah's descendant, David, king of Israel, God promised one who would reign on the throne forever:

> *When your days are fulfilled and you rest with your fathers, I will set up your seed after you, who will come from your body, and I will establish his kingdom. He shall build a house for My name, and I will establish the throne of his kingdom forever. I will be his Father, and he shall be My son. If he commits iniquity, I will chasten him with the rod of men and with the blows of the sons of men. But My mercy shall not depart from him, as I took it from Saul, whom I removed from before you. And your house and your kingdom shall be established forever before you. Your throne shall be established forever. (2 Samuel 7:12-16)*

Matthew's Gospel is written to a Jewish audience and addresses Jewish concerns, so he begins with the lineage of Jesus, establishing the succession of kingship from David. This is through the line of Joseph, whom Matthew identifies, significantly, as "the husband of Mary, of whom was born Jesus who is called Christ" (Matthew 1:16). Joseph was not the *natural* father of Jesus—the Gospel of Luke tells us that Jesus was conceived of the Holy Spirit (Luke 1:35)—but he was the *legal* father for the purposes of royal succession. In this way, Matthew demonstrates that Jesus is the King who fulfills the promise of God to David, and His kingdom fulfills the promise God made to Abraham.

In Matthew 2, wise men come to Jerusalem asking, "Where is He who has been born King of the Jews? For we have seen His star in the East" (v. 2). They know the prophecy of Numbers 24:17, "A Star shall come out of Jacob, a Scepter shall rise out of Israel." They know He is born in Bethlehem, citing Micah 5:2, "But you, Bethlehem, in the land of Judah, are not the least among the rulers of Judah; for out of you shall come a Ruler, who will shepherd My people Israel." Herod is opposed to this new King and tries to destroy Him.

Matthew 3 introduces us to John the Baptizer. He comes preaching, "Repent, for the kingdom of heaven is at hand" (v. 2). His is a baptism of repentance and many are coming to receive it. Pharisees and Sadducees come to see what he is doing. John thunders at them:

> *Brood of vipers! Who warned you to flee from the wrath to come? Therefore bear fruits worthy of repentance, and do not think to say to yourselves, "We have Abraham as our father." For I say to you that God is able to raise up children to Abraham from these stones. And even now the ax is laid to the root of the trees. Therefore every tree which does not bear good fruit is cut down and thrown into the fire.*
>
> *I indeed baptize you with water unto repentance, but He who is coming after me is mightier than I, whose sandals I am not worthy to carry. He will baptize you with the Holy Spirit and fire. His winnowing fan is in His hand, and He will thoroughly clean out His threshing floor, and gather His wheat into the barn, but He will burn up the chaff with unquenchable fire. (Matthew 3:7-12)*

The hypocrisy of these religious leaders is well known to John and he warns them of the coming wrath. The theme of their hypocrisy and judgment will continue throughout the Gospel of Matthew as the opposition of the Pharisees and Sadducees increases, for Jesus has come to baptize His people with the Holy Spirit and judge whatever does not belong to Him.

Jesus goes to John to be baptized. John resists, saying, "I need to be baptized by You, and are You coming to me?" (v. 14). Jesus answers, "Permit it to be so now, for thus it is fitting for us to fulfill all righteousness" (v. 15). He has come to identify with His people and undo Adam's disobedience—to fulfill all righteousness for our sake. John acquiesces.

> *When He had been baptized, Jesus came up immediately from the water; and behold, the heavens were opened to Him, and He saw the Spirit of*

God descending like a dove and alighting upon Him. And suddenly a voice came from heaven, saying, "This is My beloved Son, in whom I am well pleased." (Matthew 3:16-17)

In the baptism of Jesus, the veil between heaven and earth parts and the Father's voice sounds forth into the world. His declaration is full of messianic and kingly significance. "This is My beloved Son," evokes Psalm 2, about how nations and kings rage against the LORD and His Anointed, but God establishes His Messiah on the throne anyway."

"Yet I have set My King
On My holy hill of Zion."
I will declare the decree:
The LORD has said to Me,
"You are My Son,
Today I have begotten You.
Ask of Me, and I will give You
The nations for Your inheritance,
And the ends of the earth for Your possession.
You shall break them with a rod of iron;
You shall dash them to pieces like a potter's vessel."

(Psalm 2:6-9)

"In whom I am well pleased," echoes the prophecy of Isaiah:

Behold! My Servant whom I uphold,
My Elect One in whom My soul delights!
I have put My Spirit upon Him;
He will bring forth justice to the Gentiles.

(Isaiah 42:1-2)

After baptism, Jesus is led by the Spirit, who is now upon Him, up into the wilderness to be tested by the devil. The devil offers Him solutions that are easy, but wrong; he wants to stop the Messiah and ruin the plan of God. If Jesus will bow down and worship him, he promises to give Him all the kingdoms of the world—isn't that why He came, to be king? Jesus answers, "Away with you, Satan! For it is written, 'You shall worship the LORD your God, and Him only you shall serve'" (v. 10). It is not just a kingdom Jesus seeks, or even many kingdoms, but a kingdom of *righteousness*.

Jesus returns from the wilderness in victory and begins His ministry. His message is simple: "Repent, for the kingdom of heaven is at hand." It is the Gospel of the Kingdom, the good news that the rule and reign of God is now here, present in the person of the King. It is the message of Heaven on Earth.

In the following sections, we will consider the nature and dynamics of the kingdom Jesus established, the kingdom of Heaven on Earth, and how to live and operate effectively in its dominion. This is a motivational commentary on select passages in the Gospel of Matthew, to stir up your passion for the reality of God's kingdom now at work in the world.

THE SERMON OF
HEAVEN ON EARTH

The Sermon of Heaven on Earth

And Jesus went about all Galilee, teaching in their synagogues, preaching the gospel of the kingdom, and healing all kinds of sickness and all kinds of disease among the people. Then His fame went through all Syria; and they brought to Him all sick people who were afflicted with various diseases and torments, and those who were demon-possessed, epileptics and paralytics; and He healed them. Great multitudes followed Him. (Matthew 4:23-25)

Jesus came preaching the gospel of the kingdom, that the kingdom of God was now at hand, Heaven on Earth. As His fame grew throughout the region, multitudes gathered, bringing those who had various sicknesses, diseases and afflictions, the demon-possessed, the epileptics and the paralytics—and Jesus healed them all, demonstrating that the kingdom of heaven was truly present on earth.

And seeing the multitudes, He went up on a mountain, and when He was seated His disciples came to Him. Then He opened His mouth and taught them. (Matthew 5:1-2)

The custom was for Jewish teachers to sit down as they taught their disciples, and here were the multitudes in addition, to hear the instruction of Jesus. It is significant, since Matthew's Gospel is written for Jews, that Jesus went up on the mountain to teach the people. There is a subtle comparison here to Moses receiving the Law on Mount Sinai and delivering it to the children of Israel. Now, having announced that the kingdom of heaven was present on earth, Jesus goes up on the mountain and begins to elaborate on what that kingdom is all about.

THE BLESSING OF HEAVEN ON EARTH

Jesus begins with what we call the Beatitudes. It is not a short course in ethics, a checklist of *do's* and *don'ts*, as some have supposed. Book-ended by the declaration of the kingdom of heaven (verses 3 and 10), it is a pronouncement of blessing—supreme bliss and happiness—on all to whom that kingdom comes.

- *Blessed are the poor in spirit, for theirs is the kingdom of heaven* (v. 3). The kingdom belongs to those who are poor in spirit, those who trust in God alone.
- *Blessed are those who mourn, for they shall be comforted* (v. 4). The kingdom brings comfort, encouragement and hope for those who mourn over sin and its consequences.
- *Blessed are the meek, for they shall inherit the earth* (v. 5). The meek, who are not proud and arrogant but live humbly before God, inherit the earth from our Father in heaven. For the kingdom of God is not for heaven only, but also for earth.
- *Blessed are those who hunger and thirst for righteousness* (v. 6). The kingdom brings fullness and satisfaction for those who long to see righteousness done and experience it in them-selves, for it is how God's rightness is being revealed.
- *Blessed are the merciful, for they shall obtain mercy* (v. 7). The kingdom brings mercy to those who allow mercy to flow through their lives toward others.

   ‽ *Blessed are the pure in heart, for they shall see God* (v. 8). Those whose hearts are not divided but established in faith and set on God shall see Him, for it is *His* kingdom.

   ‽ *Blessed are the peacemakers, for they shall be called sons of God* (v. 9). In this kingdom, those who promote peace and goodwill are called the sons of God, for they have the wisdom that is from above (James 3:17) and show the character of God.

   ‽ *Blessed are those who are persecuted for righteousness' sake, for theirs is the kingdom of heaven* (v. 10). The kingdom belongs to those who are persecuted for the sake of God's way of doing and being right. They overcome the evil one by the blood of the Lamb, by the word of their testimony, and because they love Him more than their own lives (Revelation 12:11).

Jesus expands on the last Beatitude: "Blessed are you when they revile and persecute you, and say all kinds of evil against you falsely for My sake. Rejoice and be exceedingly glad, for great is your reward in heaven, for so they persecuted the prophets who were before you" (v. 11-12). To be persecuted for righteousness' sake is to be persecuted for His sake, and *vice versa*. The reward is great—Heaven on Earth!—for the King and His kingdom are now present.

THE SALT OF THE EARTH AND THE FLAVOR OF HEAVEN

You are the salt of the earth; but if the salt loses its flavor, how shall it be seasoned? It is then good for nothing but to be thrown out and trampled underfoot by men. (Matthew 5:13)

The Sermon of Heaven on Earth is about the kingdom of heaven— the will of God being done on earth as it is in heaven. In this verse, Jesus tells all His disciples that we are the "salt of the earth."

Salt was very important back in Biblical times (and still is today).

Not only was it vital for the body, it was used as a preservative and played an integral part in the animal sacrifices of the Old Testament (Leviticus 2:13) as the symbol of unbreakable covenant. Here in His sermon, though, Jesus focuses on salt as a seasoning.

If we are the salt of the earth, then what is to be the flavor? The kingdom of heaven. Jesus not only *preached* about the kingdom, He *demonstrated* its power to bring healing, wholeness and freedom. He brought the flavor of the kingdom—the flavor of heaven—into the world.

Jesus calls us the salt of the earth. Our job is to bring the flavor of heaven to the world, to manifest the kingdom of Heaven on Earth in all we do and say. We bring the teaching, the works and the life of Jesus Christ to the world through the preaching of the gospel and the power of the Holy Spirit. It is only through faith and obedience to Him that we retain our saltiness and bring forth the savor of heaven.

SHINING WITH THE LIGHT OF HEAVEN

You are the light of the world. A city that is set on a hill cannot be hidden. Nor do they light a lamp and put it under a basket, but on a lampstand, and it gives light to all who are in the house. Let your light so shine before men, that they may see your good works and glorify your Father in heaven. (Matthew 5:14-16)

Jesus calls us the "light of the world." That is a powerful declaration, for many reasons:

- *God is light.* "This is the message which we have heard from Him and declare to you, that God is light and in Him is no darkness at all" (1 John 1:5).
- *God is the Father of Lights.* "Every good gift and every perfect gift is from above, and comes down from the Father of Lights, with whom there is no variation or shadow of turning" (James 1:17).

- ❧ *Light overcomes the darkness.* "And the light shines in the darkness, and the darkness did not comprehend it" (John 1:5).
- ❧ *Jesus is the Light of the World,* "the true Light which gives light to every man coming into the world" (John 1:9)
- ❧ *Darkness is passing away.* "Again, a new commandment I write to you, which thing is true in Him and in you, because the darkness is passing away, and the true light is already shining" (1 John 2:8).
- ❧ *God has delivered us from darkness.* "He has delivered us from the power of darkness and conveyed us into the kingdom of the Son of His love" (Colossians 1:13).
- ❧ *God has caused the true light to shine in us.* "For it is the God who commanded light to shine out of darkness, who has shone in our hearts to give the light of the knowledge of the glory of God in the face of Jesus Christ" (2 Corinthians 4:6).
- ❧ *God has made us light in the Lord.* "For you were once darkness, but now you are light in the Lord. Walk as children of light" (Ephesians 5:8).

As believers in Jesus Christ, we are the light of the world. We shine with the light that comes from the Father through the Son. It is the light of the knowledge of the glory of God seen in the face of Jesus Christ. This light is for all the world. Before He ascended to heaven, Jesus gave this command to His disciples:

All authority has been given to Me in heaven and on earth. Go therefore and make disciples of all the nations, baptizing them in the name of the Father and of the Son and of the Holy Spirit, teaching them to observe all things that I have commanded you; and lo, I am with you always, even to the end of the age. (Matthew 28:18-20)

Go into all the world and preach the gospel to every creature. He who believes and is baptized will be saved; but he who does not believe will be condemned. And these signs will follow those who believe: In My name they will cast out demons; they will speak with new tongues; they will take up serpents; and if they drink anything deadly, it will by no means hurt them; they will lay hands on the sick, and they will recover. (Mark 16:15-18)

You shall receive power when the Holy Spirit has come upon you; and you shall be witnesses to Me in Jerusalem, and in all Judea and Samaria, and to the end of the earth. (Acts 1:8)

Jesus, Light of the World, authorizes us to take His light into all the world. He supplies us with the power to overcome the darkness and shine for Him. He does not intend for us to be hidden away but to be set up on a lampstand and as a city on a hill, so that everyone on earth can benefit from the light and give glory to our Father in heaven. For the light is of Him, and heaven is where it is from.

The Certainty of Heaven on Earth

Do not think that I came to destroy the Law or the Prophets. I did not come to destroy but to fulfill. For assuredly, I say to you, till heaven and earth pass away, one jot or one tittle will by no means pass from the law till all is fulfilled. (Matthew 5:17-18)

Nothing in Jesus' words or acts should ever be taken as setting aside or breaking anything in the Law or Prophets. Quite the opposite, for Jesus was announcing that He is the *fulfillment* of all that was required by the Law and foretold by the Prophets. The focus of the Old Testament promise was on the coming of Messiah and the establishment of God's kingdom. Jesus is the realization. He is the Christ, the Messiah, anointed by God to rule and reign, to be King over His people. His anointing sets people free from bondage and affliction, removes burdens and destroys yokes. He is the assurance that everything God promised will be fulfilled on earth as well as in heaven. His personal ministry on earth was just the beginning.

GREATNESS IN THE KINGDOM

Whoever therefore breaks one of the least of these commandments, and teaches men so, shall be called least in the kingdom of heaven; but whoever does and teaches them, he shall be called great in the kingdom of heaven. For I say to you, that unless your righteousness exceeds the righteousness of the scribes and Pharisees, you will by no means enter the kingdom of heaven. (Matthew 5:19-20)

All the Law and the Prophets are fulfilled in Jesus Christ. He is the one by whom the commandments are given their proper understanding and purpose. In the natural, we are often inclined to weigh the commandments of God from the greatest to the least. The Pharisees were masters at this. But *all* of God's commandments are important to God, and so they should be to us.

The real distinction Jesus is making here, however, is not between greater and lesser acts but between outward acts and inward disposition. That is, it is a matter of the heart. It is not only the outward actions of obedience that are important; God also looks upon the inward man—the obedience of the heart (as we will see in Matthew 5:21-48). This may seem like a lesser thing to some, but if we ignore it or treat it lightly, we will be disqualified for greatness in the kingdom of heaven.

We need a righteousness that goes beyond the righteousness of the Pharisees; we need a righteousness of the heart. When we obey God with the whole heart, a heart of righteousness, we will stand among the greatest in His kingdom.

This requires a work of God; we cannot do it on our own. That is why Jesus came. God made Him "who knew no sin to be sin for us, that we might become the righteousness of God in Him" (2 Corinthians 5:21). Jesus did what we could not do: He kept the Law perfectly and fulfilled all its requirements. Then He *became* sin for us that we might *become* the righteousness of God in Him. This is more than about just giving and receiving righteousness. It is about *becoming* righteousness. It is not just about what we *have* in Him but about what we *are* in Him.

Through faith in Christ, the righteousness of God is revealed in us, in *who we are*. God gives us His Spirit so that this righteousness can be manifested by *what we do*. "The fruit of the Spirit is love, joy, peace longsuffering, kindness, goodness, faithfulness, gentleness, self-control. Against such there is no law" (Galatians 5:22-23).

Here, then, is the righteousness that exceeds that of the scribes and Pharisees. It is fulfilled in the Lord Jesus, and by Him and His Spirit, it is fulfilled in all who receive Him by faith. Here also is greatness in the kingdom of Heaven on Earth as we yield to the Spirit of God and the fruit He comes to bring forth in us.

The Kingdom of the Heart

In Matthew 5:21-48, Jesus deals with the kingdom of the heart. He comes, not to destroy the Law and the Prophets, but to fulfill them (v. 17-18). Even the "least" of the commandments are important to God (v. 19). They reveal the heart. The righteousness required by the kingdom of heaven is one that must exceed the righteousness of the Pharisees (v. 20). It is more than external acts—it requires the whole heart set on God.

In the balance of chapter 5, Jesus digs deeper and shows that mere outward obedience to the Law is not enough. Each section is introduced with this formula: "You have heard that it was said ... But I say to you ..." He applies it first to the Sixth Commandment.

MURDER IN THE HEART

You have heard that it was said to those of old, "You shall not murder, and whoever murders will be in danger of the judgment." But I say to you that whoever is angry with his brother without a cause shall be in danger of the judgment. And whoever says to his brother, "Raca!" shall be in danger of the council. But whoever says, "You fool!" shall be in danger of hell fire. (Matthew 5:21-22)

The Pharisees kept the Sixth Commandment by refraining from physically murdering others. But the purpose of God goes much deeper, as Jesus shows: If one is angry with his brother without cause, he is leaving himself open to divine judgment; even more so when, in his anger, he calls his brother unfair names (words are very important in the economy of God, for He created the world by His words). It is good that the angry man does not actually kill his brother, but the root of the unjust anger in his heart must be dealt with. Jesus presses the matter even further:

> *Therefore if you bring your gift to the altar, and there remember that your brother has something against you, leave your gift there before the altar, and go your way. First be reconciled to your brother, and then come and offer your gift.*
>
> *Agree with your adversary quickly, while you are on the way with him, lest your adversary deliver you to the judge, the judge hand you over to the officer, and you be thrown into prison. Assuredly, I say to you, you will by no means get out of there till you have paid the last penny. (Matthew 5:23-26)*

Jesus is still dealing with the divine implications of the Sixth Commandment. His point is that harmonious relationships among brothers is more important even than acts of worship. It is better to go first and be reconciled with each other, and then bring our gifts to God. The adversarial relationship in a court case provides another example: It is better to settle disputes quickly, instead of "killing" each other in court.

Murder begins in the heart, and we have many ways we unjustly "kill" each other. These must all be resolved if we are going to experience the kingdom of Heaven on Earth, for at the deepest level, it is a kingdom of the heart.

Faithfulness in the Heart

You have heard that it was said to those of old, "You shall not commit adultery." But I say to you that whoever looks at a woman to lust for her has already committed adultery with her in his heart. (Matthew 5:27-28)

Now Jesus is dealing with the Seventh Commandment. In the divine purpose, it is about more than simply refraining from the physical act of adultery. It concerns faithfulness in the heart. The heart is not only the center of the emotions but also of the intellect and the will. That is why Jesus speaks of intent: "Whoever looks at a woman *to lust for* her." The problem is not that stray thoughts slip through but that they are entertained. As someone has said, you cannot stop a bird from flying over your head but you *can* keep it from building a nest in your hair. When a man or woman looks with intent and gives way to lust, they have broken the commandment of God, committing adultery in their heart.

If your right eye causes you to sin, pluck it out and cast it from you; for it is more profitable for you that one of your members perish, than for your whole body to be cast into hell. And if your right hand causes you to sin, cut it off and cast it from you; for it is more profitable for you that one of your members perish, than for your whole body to be cast into hell. (Matthew 5:29-30)

The Greek word for "offend" is *skandalizo* and refers to that which would ensnare you or become a stumbling block that causes you to fall into sin. Jesus is not counseling that one should literally gouge out his eye or cut off his hand. The eye and the hand do not act independently of the heart; to remove them would not solve anything. The point is that one must be diligent to deal with the problem at the root, however painful it may be. We must address the heart and its affections, and that is often the more difficult thing to do, which goes to show how much we need God.

Furthermore it has been said, "Whoever divorces his wife, let him give her a certificate of divorce." But I say to you that whoever divorces his wife for any reason except sexual immorality causes her to commit adultery; and whoever marries a woman who is divorced commits adultery. (Matthew 5:31-32)

There was a school of rabbinic thought which allowed a man to divorce his wife for virtually any reason at all. In Jesus' eyes, that was no better than committing adultery, for there is no love or commitment in that, no faithfulness of the heart. But that is always what God is looking for—the faithful disposition of the heart. The kingdom of Heaven on Earth requires it.

HONESTY IN THE HEART

Again you have heard that it was said to those of old, "You shall not swear falsely, but shall perform your oaths to the Lord." But I say to you, do not swear at all: neither by heaven, for it is God's throne; nor by the earth, for it is His footstool; nor by Jerusalem, for it is the city of the great King. Nor shall you swear by your head, because you cannot make one hair white or black. But let your "Yes" be "Yes," and your "No," "No." For whatever is more than these is from the evil one. (Matthew 5:33-37)

This section has do with the Third Commandment, "You shall not take the name of the LORD your God in vain, for the LORD will not hold him guiltless who takes His name in vain" (Exodus 20:7); and the Ninth, "You shall not bear false witness" (Exodus 20:16).

It was commonly understood that vows made to God and oaths made in the name of the Lord could not be broken. But another understanding had also developed that one could swear by lesser things, such as by heaven, earth, Jerusalem, the Temple or the altar, and such oaths would not be as binding. We see examples of this toward the end of Matthew's Gospel, where Jesus rebukes the Scribes and Pharisees for this very practice.

Woe to you, blind guides, who say, "Whoever swears by the temple, it is nothing; but whoever swears by the gold of the temple, he is obliged to perform it." Fools and blind! For which is greater, the gold or the temple that sanctifies the gold?

And, "Whoever swears by the altar, it is nothing; but whoever swears by the gift that is on it, he is obliged to perform it." Fools and blind! For which is greater, the gift or the altar that sanctifies the gift?

Therefore he who swears by the altar, swears by it and by all things on it. He who swears by the temple, swears by it and by Him who dwells in it. And he who swears by heaven, swears by the throne of God and by Him who sits on it. (Matthew 23:16-22)

In both places, Jesus makes the point that if you swear by whatever belongs to God, you are swearing by God Himself, so the oaths are just as binding, and whoever breaks them will be just as guilty. One cannot swear even by one's own head without swearing by God, for we cannot naturally make one hair of our head turn black or white—that is in God's hands.

Jesus does away completely with the system of false swearing and making oaths on supposedly lesser things. It was never anything more than a tactic to leave room for a lie when the truth became too inconvenient. So here again was the attempt to keep the commandments outwardly, not with the whole heart.

Jesus' solution is simple: Let your *yes* be *yes* and your *no* be *no*. In other words, give an honest answer. Say what you mean and mean what you say. That will not only fulfill the commandment but also God's purpose in the commandment. It is the only honest way; anything other than that comes from the evil one, who is the "father of lies" (John 8:44). The kingdom of Heaven on Earth requires honesty in the heart.

A Heart Free of Vengeance

You have heard that it was said, "An eye for an eye and a tooth for a tooth." But I tell you not to resist an evil person. But whoever slaps you on your

right cheek, turn the other to him also. If anyone wants to sue you and take
away your tunic, let him have your cloak also. And whoever compels you
to go one mile, go with him two. Give to him who asks you, and from him
who wants to borrow from you do not turn away. (Matthew 5:38-42)

The Law of Moses allowed, in cases of injury or loss, for a penalty to be applied in proportion to that injury or loss (see Exodus 21:23-25). For example, a man who lost an eye because of the wrongful action of another had a right to receive amends or compensation for the loss of that eye, but not in excess of that eye. Or, a man who similarly lost a tooth had a right to be compensated for the loss of that tooth, but not as if he had lost a mouthful of teeth. This principle, known as *lex talionis* (the "law of retaliation"), is the basis for the modern tort system in which a person may sue to be compensated for wrongful loss or damage.

That is the outward working of the Law, but here Jesus is going beyond what is required to again address the inward attitude of the heart. His comments must be understood in this context. For example, when He tells us not to resist an evil person, He is not saying that we should never defend ourselves or our families against harm, and He is certainly not suggesting that a community or state should ever accept evil (indeed, Paul tells us that God establishes governing authorities for the purpose of standing against evil; Romans 13:3). Nor is He teaching that we should not oppose sin, moral evil or the devil. Rather, the "evil person" is the one who has wrongfully injured us—we are not to take it upon ourselves to exact vengeance.

"Turn to him the other [cheek] also," does not mean that we should not seek to get ourselves out of abusive situations, or that we must end-lessly put up with insult. Rather, we should not be easily provoked, but patient in endurance, slow to anger. In context, it means that we should not be quick to take the offender to court.

"If anyone wants to sue you and take away your tunic, let him have your cloak also." Don't be quick to sue someone else. But what if someone wants to sue you? Seek a better solution. Ligation often brings out anger and bitterness in people. It is better to settle with your opponent, even at a loss, rather than lose your joy, peace of mind, and the perspective of love.

Notice the subtle shift here. The Law allows for retaliation; Jesus teaches that we should be more ready to give beyond what is required than to extract all that is allowed. "Whoever compels you to go one mile, go with him two. Give to him who asks you, and from him who wants to borrow from you do not turn away." As Matthew Henry commented about this passage, "The law of retaliation must be made consistent with the law of love." Paul catches the spirit of this well:

Do not repay evil for evil. (Romans 12:17)

Do not avenge yourselves, but rather give place to wrath [i.e., let God take care of it]; for it is written, "Vengeance is mine, I will repay," says the Lord. (Romans 12:19)

Do not be overcome by evil, but overcome evil with good. (Romans 12:21)

More will be accomplished by love than by litigation, and by a generous spirit than by a heart full of vengeance. The kingdom of Heaven on Earth requires a generous heart that is free of vengeance.

A HEART THAT FREELY LOVES

You have heard that it was said, "You shall love your neighbor and hate your enemy." But I say to you, love your enemies, bless those who curse you, do good to those who hate you, and pray for those who spitefully use you and persecute you, that you may be sons of your Father in heaven; for He makes His sun rise on the evil and on the good, and sends rain on the just and on the unjust. For if you love those who love you, what reward have you? Do not even the tax collectors do the same? And if you greet your brethren only, what do you do more than others? Do not even the tax collectors do so? Therefore you shall be perfect, just as your Father in heaven is perfect. (Matthew 5:43-48)

In the previous section, Jesus talked about the payback of justice; in this section, He talks about the payback of love. But just as in the previous section He called for a heart that goes beyond trading penalty for injury, in this section He calls for a heart that goes beyond love as a *tit for tat* proposition.

The commandment to love your neighbor (Leviticus 19:18) says nothing about hating your enemy; that was incorrectly inferred from the text by rabbinical tradition. Jesus blasts that out of the water by teaching us to love even our enemies, to bless even those who curse us, to do good even to those who hate us, and pray even for those who spitefully use us. This is the way of our Father in heaven and therefore the way of the kingdom of Heaven on Earth.

Fallen human nature always desires to reciprocate, to hate those who hate us, curse those who curse us, persecute those who persecute us. It is relatively easy to love those who love us, bless those who bless us and do good to those who do good to us. But Jesus teaches us to put away the scorecard; our job is not to go around evening things up. He calls us instead to do something radically different, out of balance, and even unfair—to love those who are our enemies.

This is the way of our Father in heaven, who graciously allows the blessings of sunshine and rain to fall on both the just and the unjust. God is love, and it is the nature of love to give and serve. "But God demonstrates His own love toward us, in that while we were still sinners, Christ died for us" (Romans 5:8). It is the way of perfection, of coming into maturity and completeness, fulfilling the purpose of the Father in bringing us into His family. The pathway of Heaven on Earth is a heart that freely loves.

The Kingdom of Authentic Living

Take heed that you do not do your charitable deeds before men, to be seen by them. Otherwise you have no reward from your Father in heaven. (Matthew 6:1)

The earliest Greek manuscripts do not have the word for "charitable deeds" here but the word for "righteousness." That is why the *NASB* translates this as "Beware of practicing your *righteousness* before men to be noticed by them." The word for "to be seen," is an interesting one in this context. It is the verb *theaomai*. As a noun form, it is *theatron*, which is where we get the English word "theatre."

This verse serves as an introduction for the next three sections regarding the acts of charity, prayer and fasting. In each section, Jesus warns us not to be like the "hypocrites." The Greek word is *hypokrites* and refers literally to actors, those who pretend, play a role and wear a mask. The venue for actors, of course, is the theatre where they can be put on display to please the audience.

Jesus is speaking to the motivations of the heart. Giving alms, praying and fasting were basic acts of Jewish piety and were to be encouraged. However, they were not ends in themselves and were not to be performed with great outward display but simply and sincerely from the heart.

For those who wanted to make a show of their piety, to be seen by men for their deeds, such display would be all the reward they would receive—empty and fleeting fame. There would be no reward for them with God, who does not look only at the outward appearance, but upon the heart.

The kingdom of Heaven on Earth requires authentic living—authentic charity, authentic prayer, authentic fasting.

AUTHENTIC CHARITY

Therefore, when you do a charitable deed, do not sound a trumpet before you as the hypocrites do in the synagogues and in the streets, that they may have glory from men. Assuredly, I say to you, they have their reward. But when you do a charitable deed, do not let your left hand know what your right hand is doing, that your charitable deed may be in secret; and your Father who sees in secret will Himself reward you openly. (Matthew 6:2-4)

The Greek word for "charitable deed" here is the word for "alms." It speaks of compassion and beneficence. The purpose is to help the poor, not to receive the applause of men. The Bible says, "He who has pity on the poor lends to the LORD, and He will pay back what he has given" (Proverbs 19:17). When the Lord pays back, it is with great blessing. But if we do our alms in order to be seen by others, their acclaim will be all we have—and they have a very short attention span. We will already have reaped what we have sown, and there will be no reward from God.

Two Bible accounts show a dramatic contrast in motivations and their rewards. The first is the story of the widow's mites:

Now Jesus sat opposite the treasury and saw how the people put money into the treasury. And many who were rich put in much. Then one poor widow came and threw in two mites, which make a quadrans. So He called His

disciples to Himself and said to them, "Assuredly, I say to you that this poor
widow has put in more than all those who have given to the treasury; for
they all put in out of their abundance, but she out of her poverty put in
all that she had, her whole livelihood." (Mark 12:41-44)

This woman gave with no fanfare. It was only two mites, smaller than a penny and worth even less; it would not even make a sound as it fell into the box. But Jesus knew something about this widow and her gift that made all the difference: It was all she had. Others gave out of their abundance; she gave out of her lack—but also out of great faith. The synagogue crowd did not notice, but the Father did and He has rewarded her ever since. We do not have her name, but we remember her even today as the woman who humbly gave all she had.

Now think of Ananias and Sapphira (Acts 5:1-10). Others in their young Christian community were selling properties and laying the proceeds to the apostles' feet. This was not a requirement, but purely voluntary. Ananias and Sapphira did not have to sell any of their possessions but were free to do with them as they wished. But they wanted the admiration of the people around them, so they decided to sell a property and pretend that they were bringing all the gain to the apostles, when in fact they were holding some of it back. Again, they were free to keep any or all of the money, but they wanted to have the glory of the crowd for giving it all. So they faked it. They were *hypokrites*, stage-players in a little theater of their own devising. For a few very brief moments, they enjoyed the spotlight. But when they were soon found out, things did not end well for them. We *do* know *their* names, and for almost two thousand years they have served as a warning to hypocrites and glory-hounds. For the kingdom of Heaven on Earth requires authentic charity.

AUTHENTIC PRAYER

And when you pray, you shall not be like the hypocrites. For they love to
pray standing in the synagogues and on the corners of the streets, that they

*may be seen by men. Assuredly, I say to you, they have their reward. But
you, when you pray, go into your room, and when you have shut your
door, pray to your Father who is in the secret place; and your Father who
sees in secret will reward you openly. (Matthew 6:5-6)*

Jesus was not banning public prayer meetings. He was putting a check
on the motives of the heart. If we are doing it to be seen by men,
to show off our devotion, we are simply play-acting, hypocrites. The
satisfaction it brings, if any, will quickly evaporate and we will have
nothing left to show for it. James pegged it pretty well: "You ask and
do not receive, because you ask amiss, that you may spend it on your
pleasures" (James 4:3).

God has no regard for prayer that arises from the actor's repertoire.
He is looking for prayer that comes from the secret place of the heart,
the place where we are most able to be ourselves, to be open and honest
before God and pour ourselves out to Him. Authentic prayer is about
personal relationship, not public performance.

*And when you pray, do not use vain repetitions as the heathen do. For
they think that they will be heard for their many words. Therefore do not
be like them. For your Father knows the things you have need of before you
ask Him. (Matthew 6:7-8)*

The Greek word for "heathen" is *ethnikoi* and refers to the Gentiles, the nations, the pagans, who had no covenant with God. "Vain
repetitions" speaks of babbling, spouting meaningless words, without
thought—and without faith. Pagan prayers regularly piled up many
words and names for their deities, hoping to get divine notice. But the
idea that such mindless multiplication of prayers and words was effective
with God had also begun to slip into Jewish devotional practice.

Regardless of how many times they are repeated, words without faith
do nothing to please God. "For without faith it is impossible to please
Him, for he who comes to God must believe that He is, and that He

is a rewarder of those who diligently seek Him" (Hebrews 11:6). Jesus said that we shall have to give account for every idle word at the day of judgment (Matthew 12:36). As Martin Luther wisely put it, "The fewer words, the better prayer." But let them be faith-filled words. These are the kind of prayers God answers, for the kingdom of Heaven on Earth requires authentic prayer.

THE PRAYER OF HEAVEN ON EARTH

In this manner, therefore, pray:

> *Our Father in heaven, hallowed be Your name.*
> *Your kingdom come; Your will be done on earth as it is in heaven.*
> *Give us this day our daily bread.*
> *And forgive us our debts, as we forgive our debtors.*
> *And do not lead us into temptation, but deliver us from the evil one.*
> *For Yours is the kingdom and the power and the glory forever. Amen.*
> *(Matthew 6:9-13)*

Jesus teaches us to pray, not to be seen of men as the hypocrites do, nor with magic and manipulation like the heathen, but simply, directly, secretly and from the heart. This is the kind of prayer that honors God and opens heaven. It is the kind the Father regards and rewards.

"In this manner, therefore, pray." Jesus gives us a model prayer. It is not to be prayed by rote but with understanding and faith. It is a *way* of praying that checks our motives and calibrates our hearts, lining us up with the heart of God. The lines are simple, yet profound, and serve as a springboard for meditation and a profitable devotional life. But more than that, it is a way of praying that is powerful and world-changing.

This way is generally known as "The Lord's Prayer," but is sometimes regarded as "The Disciples' Prayer" because it is how Jesus taught His disciples to pray. I call it "The Prayer of Heaven on Earth" because it is about the kingdom of heaven being manifested in the here and now.

- *Our Father in heaven, hallowed be Your name.* This kind of prayer seeks, not our own glory but that of our heavenly Father. It is about His unique greatness and goodness being made known, God revealing Himself on earth.

- *Your kingdom come; Your will be done on earth as it is in heaven.* The kingdom of God is His rule and reign, His will being done on earth as it is in heaven. When things on earth are out of joint with heaven, we have authority to pray for them to line up with the will of the Father.

- *Give us this day our daily bread.* "Daily bread" is literally the "bread of the coming day," the bread of tomorrow. In the context of the coming kingdom, it is speaking of the provision of that day when God's reign is fully revealed on earth. In the meantime, we can receive that provision as we need it.

- *And forgive us our debts, as we forgive our debtors.* This is a revealer of hearts, of God's as well as our own. We are forgiven by our Father in heaven, but He also requires us to forgive our brother on earth. This may well be our hardest task, and Jesus will have more to say about it.

- *And do not lead us into temptation, but deliver us from the evil one.* Jesus came to destroy the devil and all his works (Hebrews 2:14; 1 John 3:8). "Temptation" is a test or trial. God promises that there is no temptation or trial that will be too great for us but that He will always give us a way of escape (1 Corinthians 10:13). This prayer lays hold of that escape and the victory Jesus has won for us over the evil one.

- *For Yours is the kingdom and the power and the glory forever. Amen.* Here again, it is *God's* kingdom, *God's* power and *God's* glory in view, on earth as it is in heaven.

Jesus straightens out our priorities and motivations by teaching us how to pray for the kingdom of heaven to manifest on earth.

Authentic Prayer Requires a Forgiving Heart

For if you forgive men their trespasses, your heavenly Father will also forgive you. But if you do not forgive men their trespasses, neither will your Father forgive your trespasses. (Matthew 6:14-15)

The prayer model Jesus gave His disciples said, "Forgive us our debts, as we forgive our debtors." Now He gives the matter special attention. Unwillingness to forgive is one of the most powerful hindrances to prayer. Eugene Peterson, in *The Message*, gives his commentary on this passage: "In prayer there is a connection between what God does and what you do. You can't get forgiveness from God, for instance, without also forgiving others."

Jesus also addresses unforgiveness in another place, in the same context where He teaches the disciples about prayer and the faith that moves mountains:

Have faith in God. For assuredly, I say to you, whoever says to this mountain, "Be removed and be cast into the sea," and does not doubt in his heart, but believes that those things he says will be done, he will have whatever he says. Therefore I say to you, whatever things you ask when you pray, believe that you receive them, and you will have them. And whenever you stand praying, if you have anything against anyone, forgive him, that your Father in heaven may also forgive you your trespasses. (Mark 11:22-25)

As powerful and effective as prayer and faith are, even to the moving of mountains, if we do not forgive others, we are not in a position for God to hear us. When we do not forgive others, we are still in unrepentance and not yet ready to receive forgiveness. But when we learn to forgive, we are better able to hear the Father's heart and pray in agreement with it. For His desire is to forgive, and when we pray in agreement with His will, we can know that He hears us, and knowing that He hears us, we can know that we will receive whatever we ask (1 John 5:14-15). Authentic prayer requires a forgiving heart.

Authentic Fasting

Moreover, when you fast, do not be like the hypocrites, with a sad countenance. For they disfigure their faces that they may appear to men to be fasting. Assuredly, I say to you, they have their reward. But you, when you fast, anoint your head and wash your face, so that you do not appear to men to be fasting, but to your Father who is in the secret place; and your Father who sees in secret will reward you openly. (Matthew 6:16-18)

When the hypocrites were fasting, they really wanted to look like they were fasting. For them, that was the whole point. If they could have gotten away with looking like they were fasting without actually having to fast, for them, that might have served just as well.

At the beginning of His sermon, Jesus spoke comfort to those who mourn, that is, those who are grieved by sin and injustice. Fasting is a natural counterpart to mourning. He also declared blessing on those who hunger and thirst for righteousness—they shall be filled. That is the kind of fast that God rewards, as He said through the prophet Isaiah:

Is this not the fast that I have chosen:
*   To loose the bonds of wickedness,*
To undo the heavy burdens,
*   To let the oppressed go free,*
*   And that you break every yoke?*
Is it not to share your bread with the hungry,
*   And that you bring to your house the poor who are cast out;*
When you see the naked, that you cover him,
*   And not hide yourself from your own flesh?*
Then your light shall break forth like the morning,
*   Your healing shall spring forth speedily,*
And your righteousness shall go before you;
*   The glory of the LORD shall be your rear guard.*

Then you shall call, and the LORD will answer;
You shall cry, and He will say, "Here I am."

(Isaiah 58:6-9)

This is not a fast of sad countenances and facial contortions. It is not religious theater, a "Pious Playhouse" production. It is a fast that begins in the heart. When we fast to become more mindful of God's priorities, so that we may better hear and obey His voice, it honors Him, and He honors it.

It is not hard to look like you are fasting when you actually are. The real trick is to look like you are not, and that will help you keep your motives clear. The kingdom of Heaven on Earth requires authentic fasting—the hunger and thirst for righteousness.

The Treasure of Heaven on Earth

Do not lay up for yourselves treasures on earth, where moth and rust destroy and where thieves break in and steal; but lay up for yourselves treasures in heaven, where neither moth nor rust destroys and where thieves do not break in and steal. For where your treasure is, there your heart will be also. (Matthew 6:19-21)

Jesus is not just talking about what you do with your disposable income, the money left over after you have paid all your bills. He is not making an appeal at offering time (which is the only way some preachers know how to use this verse). No, He is doing something far more reaching. Something radical, in fact. He is getting down to the root of how we live our lives, the priorities we make and the things we value. He is really speaking about the treasure of our hearts, and there are three decisions we must make:

- ❧ We must choose where we will lay up our treasure—on earth or in heaven.
- ❧ We must choose whether our eye will be evil or good, whether we will be greedy or generous.
- ❧ We must choose which master we will serve—God or mammon.

Treasure in the Kingdom

Jesus said, "*Stop* laying up for yourselves treasures on earth." That is the force of His statement: *Stop*! There is to be no more of it at all. Why? Because it does not last. It is easily corrupted and quickly fades away, and in the end, we will find that we have been robbed.

The Greek word for "treasure" is *thesauros*. The Septuagint, which is a very early Greek translation of the Old Testament, uses *thesauros* to translate the Hebrew word for "storehouse." Jesus is literally saying, "Stop storing up for yourselves *storehouses* on earth."

As important as it is to notice what Jesus *is* saying, it is just as important to note what He is *not* saying. He is not telling us to stop laying up treasure for ourselves, for He goes on to say, "But lay up *for yourselves* treasures in heaven." He wants us to have storehouses, and God promises to "command the blessing" on the storehouses of those who honor Him and keep His commandments (Deuteronomy 28:8). Rather, it is the *purpose* of our storehouses that must change. We must start operating in the purpose of the kingdom of God, the will of God being done on earth as it is in heaven. It requires everything we are and have, but it brings great reward, as Jesus shows us in this brief parable:

> *Again, the kingdom of heaven is like treasure hidden in a field, which a man found and hid; and for joy over it he goes and sells all that he has and buys that field. (Matthew 13:44)*

The kingdom of heaven is like a treasure, a storehouse full of wonderful things. But notice where it is hidden: "in a field," that is, on earth. This treasure is *from* heaven but it is *on* earth.

What is a storehouse and what is its purpose? A storehouse is a place where resources are kept until they are needed. Having a storehouse is a prudent plan for the future. The future in view here, however, is not about when we depart this life and enter the next. We do not really need to store up anything for *that* life where everything has already been well supplied. It is in *this* life that we need the resources of heaven. Laying up treasure for ourselves in heaven is about basing the provision we need for this life on the economy of heaven.

This was not a new concept; it had long been a part of Jewish understanding. Compare the words of Jesus with these ancient Hebrew writings of the Old Testament era.

Lay up your treasure according to the commandments of the Most High, and it will profit you more than gold. Store up almsgiving in your treasury, and it will rescue you from every disaster. (Sirach 29:11-12 NRSV)

Give alms from your possession, and do not let your eye begrudge the gift when you make it. Do not turn your face away from anyone who is poor, and the face of God will not be turned away from you. If you have many possessions, make your gift from them in proportion; if few, do not be afraid to give according to the little you have. So you will be laying up a good treasure for yourself against the day of necessity. (Tobit 4:7-10 NRSV)

It was common in those days for people to store up their supply in jars and bury them in the ground until needed. The problem, as Jesus pointed out, was that such materials could become corrupted or stolen. Ancient Jewish wisdom, therefore, reminded them to hedge themselves against disaster and necessity by a very counterintuitive means: Giving to the poor. Those who give alms are banking on the economy of heaven. God does not forget but rewards those who do, taking care of them in their time of need.

In his letter to Timothy, the apostle Paul addresses the theme of laying up treasure and establishes the proper perspective:

Command those who are rich in this present age not to be haughty, nor to trust in uncertain riches but in the living God, who gives us richly all things to enjoy. Let them do good, that they be rich in good works, ready to give, willing to share, storing up for themselves a good foundation for the time *to come, that they may lay hold on eternal life.* (1 Timothy 6:17-19)*

"Laying up treasure" is a matter of the heart, for "where your treasure is, there will your heart be also." The priorities of your life and the things you value will be reflected in everything you do and all you have. Will it reveal the corruptions of earth or the glories of Heaven on Earth? Store up for yourself treasure in the kingdom of heaven, and it will be a blessing, to you as well as others, on earth.

THE GOOD EYE

The lamp of the body is the eye. If therefore your eye is good, your whole body will be light. But if your eye is bad, your whole body will be full of darkness. If therefore the light that is in you is darkness, how great is that darkness! (Matthew 6:22-23)

Jesus is not giving us an anatomy lesson here; He is still talking about laying up treasure. Just as we must choose where we will store up our treasure (on earth or in heaven), we must also choose whether our eye will be evil or good. Speaking of the eye in this way, Jesus is using an ancient Hebrew idiom that describes whether a man is generous or greedy. We see an example of the "evil eye" in the book of Proverbs:

A man with an evil eye hastens after riches,
  And does not consider that poverty will come upon him.
                                              (Proverbs 28:22)

The man with an evil eye loves money. It has become his master and

---

he trusts in it to see him through. What he does not realize is that he is actually on the road to poverty and ruin. We discover the source of the evil eye in the book of Deuteronomy:

> *Beware lest there be a wicked thought in your heart saying, "The seventh year, the year of release is at hand," and your eye be evil against your poor brother and you give him nothing, and he cry out to the LORD against you, and it become sin among you. (Deuteronomy 15:9)*

The evil eye of stinginess starts as a wicked thought in the heart. The Hebrew word for "wicked" is *belial* and refers to that which is destructive, worthless, profitless. It does not add to the goodness of life but takes away from it. The man with the evil eye is deceived to think he will profit by his greed. He will not even break even but will lose all he has. That is why Jesus said, "if your eye is bad, your whole body will be full of darkness … how great is that darkness." He describes that darkness in another place:

> *For from within, out of the heart of men, proceed evil thoughts, adulteries, fornications, murders, thefts, covetousness, wickedness, deceit, lewdness, an evil eye, blasphemy, pride, foolishness. All these things come from within and defile a man. (Mark 7:21-23)*

But enough of the evil eye. Let's talk about the good eye—that's where the blessing is. Jesus said, "If therefore your eye is good, your whole body will be light." The Greek word used here for "good" literally means "without folds" or unentwined. It is simple, single, clear. The good eye is not complicated by greed, as is the evil eye. A man with a good eye is generous. He sows generously and reaps abundantly (2 Corinthians 9:6). Psalm 112 describes the blessing of such a man:

> *Blessed is the man who fears the LORD,*
> *Who delights greatly in His commandments.*

His descendants will be mighty on earth;
The generation of the upright will be blessed.
Wealth and riches will be in his house,
And his righteousness endures forever.
Unto the upright there arises light in the darkness;
He is gracious, and full of compassion, and righteous.
A good man deals graciously and lends;
He will guide his affairs with discretion …
He has dispersed abroad,
He has given to the poor;
His righteousness endures forever;
His horn will be exalted with honor.

(Psalm 112:1-5, 9)

This is a man who honors the Lord and follows His Word. It sheds light in his heart and he becomes light to all those around because he is full of grace and compassion. His generosity does not lead to poverty but to prosperity. Wealth and riches will be in his house. The greedy eye leads to lack, poverty and destruction. The generous eye leads to prosperity and honor.

ONLY ONE MASTER

No one can serve two masters; for either he will hate the one and love the other, or else he will be loyal to the one and despise the other. You cannot serve God and mammon. (Matthew 6:24)

"Mammon" is an ancient word that refers, not just to money but also to the god of money. The Greeks had Plutus as their god of money. The Jews never formalized such a deity, but there were some who idolized money just the same.

We cannot serve both God and money. For one thing, God will not share His glory with any other—the First Commandment declares, "I am the L ORD your God … you shall have no other gods before Me." For another thing, our hearts are not made to be divided. If we try to serve both God and mammon, we will end up loving one and hating the other. It is the source of great confusion in both the inward and outward realms of our lives.

It is not money itself but our attitude toward it that is the problem. Some people think the Bible teaches that money is the root of all evil, but what it actually says is that the *love* of many is the root of all evil (or all *kinds* of evil; 1 Timothy 6:10, *NKJV*). Many people love, serve and put their trust in money for their welfare. They have made it their god.

Money can be a wonderful servant but it is a tyrannical master. A rich young man came to Jesus asking, "What good thing shall I do that I may have eternal life?" He did not realize that good works do not *gain* us eternal life—they *flow out of* eternal life. After establishing that the young man knew and kept the Commandments (or thought he did), Jesus answered, "If you want to be perfect, go, sell what you have and give to the poor, and you will have treasure in heaven; and come, follow Me." Matthew says (read about this in Matthew 19:16-22), "But when the young man heard that saying, he went away sorrowful, for he had great possessions."

As it turns out, this young man failed in the very First Commandment. He did not trust in God alone and love Him with all his heart; he had already made a prior commitment to the god of money. His heart was chained to his possessions. He affected a fine religious tone but he loved and trusted in his wealth and was therefore unwilling to put all his faith in God. He could have treasured up his treasure in heaven, trusting God with everything in his life and serving Him alone—and he would have been full of joy. Instead, he remained the slave of his money, laying up his treasure on earth, and went away full of sorrow.

Who or what will you love, serve and trust? It will determine where you lay up your treasure, and whether that treasure will endure.

Seek the Kingdom, Find Everything

Therefore do not worry, saying, "What shall we eat?" or "What shall we drink?" or "What shall we wear?" For after all these things the Gentiles seek. For your heavenly Father knows that you need all these things. But seek first the kingdom of God and His righteousness, and all these things shall be added to you. (Matthew 6:31-33)

The whole world scrambles for food, clothing and shelter. The Gentiles, because they do not have a covenant with God, must do for themselves, which often leads to worry, fear, and even anger.

Worry comes from laying up treasure on earth. When we invest ourselves in thinking the way the world thinks, acting the way the world acts, believing the way the world believes, we end up worrying the way the world worries. We look to the world to meet our needs because that is where we have treasured up our lives. In our hearts, we realize how fickle the world is and fear that it will let us down—and it always does. When we learn to treasure up our treasure in heaven, all the needs we have on earth will be met and we will have more than enough so that we can bless others. "God is able to make all grace abound toward you, that you, always having all sufficiency in all things, may have an abundance for every good work" (2 Corinthians 9:8).

To those who have covenant with God, Jesus gives this priority: Seek first the kingdom of God and His righteousness. He is not telling us just to put it on our "to do" list. He is not even telling us to put it at the *top* of the list, as if we are to seek the kingdom of God first and *then* seek after the other things. No, He is saying that there is only one priority—the kingdom of God and His righteousness. When we seek that, everything else will be added to us. It will all be taken care of.

God always deals with His people on the basis of covenant, and the essence of covenant is exchange: We give Him all we are and have and He gives us all He is and has. In other words, when we belong to God, He will always take care of us. In the Old Testament, God made covenant with Abraham, and confirmed it with Isaac and Jacob. It was a covenant to bless, not only Abraham and his descendants, but also all the nations of the earth. In the New Testament, we see that this covenant is fulfilled in Jesus Christ, who is called the "Seed" of Abraham (Galatians 3:16).

> *Christ has redeemed us from the curse of the law, having become a curse for us (for it is written, "Cursed is everyone who hangs on a tree"), that the blessing of Abraham might come upon the Gentiles in Christ Jesus, that we might receive the promise of the Spirit through faith. (Galatians 3:13-14)*

The Lord Jesus is Himself the mediator of a new and better covenant, instituted in His own blood (Hebrews 8:6; Luke 22:20), and nothing is left out of it. He has provided everything we will ever need.

What does it mean to seek the kingdom of God and His righteousness? The kingdom of God is His rule and reign, His will being done on earth as it is in heaven (Matthew 6:10). God's righteousness, as the *Amplified Bible* notes, is "His way of doing and being right." Seeking is about giving ourselves totally over to God, looking for His rule and reign in everything, and obeying it. It is doing things God's way, which is the right way and will always bring the right results.

When we make the kingdom of God our one and only priority, we will not have to seek after anything else; it will all be included. It will all be taken care of, because it has already been provided for in His will. You might call it a "package deal." In his commentary on Matthew 6:33, Adam Clarke illustrates it this way:

> *This was a very common saying among the Jews: "Seek that, to which other things are necessarily connected." "A king said to his particular friend, 'Ask what thou wilt, and I will give it unto thee.' He thought within himself, 'If I ask to be made a general I shall readily obtain it. I will ask something to which all these things shall be added:' he therefore said, 'Give*

me thy daughter to wife.' This he did knowing that all the dignities of the
kingdom should be added unto this gift."

Our job—first, last and always—is to seek the rule and reign of God and His way of doing things. When we do, everything else will be added to us.

Discerning Heaven on Earth

Not everything on earth comes from heaven, and therefore does not belong to Heaven on Earth, the kingdom of God breaking into this present age. As the apostle John said, "the darkness is passing away and the true light is already shining" (1 John 2:8). However, there are still false prophets, false paths and false foundations around. So we must learn to discern between the true and the false, the good and the bad, the right and the wrong. Yet we must learn to do so without judging others unjustly and be discerning without condemning.

We are not without help in this, though, for God, who is the giver of all good gifts, gives us His Spirit and the resource of prayer. When we ask Him to lead us in the right way, He will show us. When we seek after His kingdom with all our hearts, we will find it. He will guide us to the right door, and when we knock on it, it will be opened to us. In this way, we will discern the kingdom of Heaven on Earth.

GODLY DISCERNMENT OR JUDGMENTAL SPIRIT?

Judge not, that you be not judged. For with what judgment you judge, you will be judged; and with the measure you use, it will be measured back to you. And why do you look at the speck in your brothers' eye, but do not consider the plank in your own eye? Or how can you say to your brother,

"Let me remove the speck from your eye"; and look, a plank is in your own eye? Hypocrite! First remove the plank from your own eye, and then you will see clearly to remove the speck from your brother's eye. (Matthew 7:1-5)

Jesus teaches us not to be judgmental, that is, not to be prejudiced and condemning. Condemning others is not our job. Loving them is. Everything we do and say needs to be done and said in love because God *is* love (1 John 4:8). However, this does not mean that we are not supposed to use discernment. Notice what Jesus says in Matthew 7:6.

Do not give what is holy to the dogs; nor cast your pearls before swine, lest they trample them under their feet, and turn and tear you in pieces.

To obey this command, we need to be able to discern what is holy, which are the pearls and who are the dogs and the swine. We also need to be able to discern false prophets, as we see a few verses later:

Beware of false prophets, who come to you in sheep's clothing, but inwardly they are ravenous wolves. You will know them by their fruits. Do men gather grapes from thorn bushes or figs from thistles? Even so, every good tree bears good fruit, but a bad tree bears bad fruit. (Matthew 7:15-17)

In order to discern the false prophets, we must be able to discern their fruit, whether it is good or bad, whether it comes from the Tree of Life or from the Tree of the Knowledge of Good and Evil (Genesis 2:9). The author of Hebrews tells us that, "Solid food belongs to those who are of full age, that is, those who by reason of use have their senses exercised to discern both good and evil" (Hebrews 5:14). Proper discernment is a mark of maturity in the Christian faith.

There is also a spiritual manifestation given by the Holy Spirit that is called "discernment of spirits" (1 Corinthians 12:10). It is the ability to know whether something originates from God, from satan or simply from the heart of man. The Greek word for "discernment" is *diakrino* and comes from the word used for "judge" (*krino*) in Matthew 7:1.

God is light, God is love, God is life. His way will always be about those things that shed light, manifest love and promote life. When we have God at work in us, we have light, love and life at work in us. Because of light, we have the ability to discern; because of love, we are not to condemn. The judgment of discernment promotes life; the judgment of condemnation brings death.

We must always practice discernment, and there are even times when we must declare publicly what we have discerned, but it is never right for us to condemn one another. Before we seek to discern anything else, we must first discern our own heart. For how can we help someone with a tiny speck in their eye if we have a large plank hanging out of our own? But when our heart is clear and operating in the light, love and life of God, then we will be able to see, discern and be of help.

GOD GIVES GOOD THINGS

Ask, and it will be given you; seek, and you will find; knock, and it will be opened to you. For everyone who asks receives, and he who seeks finds, and to him who knocks it will be opened. Or what man is there among you who, if his son asks for bread, will give him a stone? Or if he asks for a fish, will he give him a serpent? If you then, being evil, know how to give good gifts to your children, how much more will your Father who is in heaven give good things to those who ask Him! Therefore, whatever you want men to do to you, do also to them, for this is the Law and the Prophets. (Matthew 7:7-12)

Our way with God is always to be this: ask, seek, knock. He has already promised that we will receive what we ask, find what we seek and have the door opened to us. Why? Because God is a good Father who gives His children good things. "Every good gift and every perfect gift is from above, and comes down for the Father of lights, with whom there is no variation or shadow of turning" (James 1:17). When we go to God, we can always count on Him to give us what is good.

Always. For there is no variation or shadow of turning with Him. That is, He does not change.

> For the LORD God is a sun and shield;
> The LORD will give grace and glory;
> No good thing will He withhold
> From those who walk uprightly.
>
> (Psalm 84:11)

> [He] satisfies your mouth with good things,
> So that your youth is renewed like the eagle's.
>
> (Psalm 103:5)

God does not deceive, does not compromise, does not hold back. If we ask for bread, He will give us bread. He will not try to trick us with a stone that looks like bread. He won't try to pass off a serpent for a fish. God may work in mysterious ways but He doesn't work in deceitful or stingy ways, and He will never give us a counterfeit.

We who are fathers on earth may be flawed but we still know how to give good gifts to our children. How much more, then, will our Father in heaven, who is perfect in every way, give good things to us when we ask?

Jesus adds something else to the mix: "Therefore, whatever you want men to do to you, do also to them, for this is the Law and the Prophets." We know this as the "Golden Rule." Notice that it is preceded by the word "therefore." An old saying in Bible interpretation is that, whenever you see a "therefore," find out what it is *there for*. "Therefore" connects this to the passage on asking and receiving.

If you want to receive good things, are you willing to give good things? For our receiving comes not only from God, but from men as well. In Luke's rendering of this sermon (in the same position, following "Judge not") Jesus says this:

Give and it will be given to you; good measure, pressed down, shaken together, and running over will be put into your bosom. For with the same measure that you give, it will be measured back to you. (Luke 6:38; the *KJV* has "shall men give into your bosom")

God is a good Father who gives good things to those who ask. Therefore, ask and expect to receive good things. But remember that it will be measured back to you in proportion to the measure by which you give to others. We can be quite free to do that because we have Jesus' assurance that we will receive what we ask, find what we are seeking, and that the door will be opened wide before us.

DISCERNING THE NARROW WAY

Enter by the narrow gate; for wide is the gate and broad is the way that leads to destruction, and there are many who go in by it. Because narrow is the gate and difficult is the way which leads to life, and there are few who find it. (Matthew 7:13-14)

The world thinks there are many paths that lead to life, that the gate is wide and the way is broad. Truth is relative to them: "Whatever works for you is good for you and whatever works for me is good for me." "I'm OK, you're OK." Each becomes his own barometer for what is right. "Whatever floats your boat." "Whatever gets you there." Now it has been further reduced to a shrug of the shoulders and "Whatever."

Long ago, Jesus taught us something very different: "Narrow is the gate and difficult is the way which leads to life, and there are few who find it." Many non-Christians and nominal Christians love to quote Jesus when He says, "Judge not, that you be not judged." They do not want their "many ways" ideology to be disturbed by anyone discerning between right and wrong, truth and error, good and evil. But they ignore Jesus when He says, "Narrow is the gate, and difficult is the way." G. K. Chesterton, brilliant Christian apologist of the last century, captured this well when he said that many people reject Christianity, not because they tried it and found it lacking, but because they found it difficult and never tried it all.

"Wide is the gate and broad is the way that leads to destruction." There are many paths that lead to loss, ruin and misery. They are exceedingly easy to enter and many people pass through them. Not just heroin addicts, alcoholics, gamblers and prostitutes; they pretty much know they are messed up, and the bitterness of their way is very near the surface of their lives. But also politicians, corporate executives, university professors, even church leaders. So many of them have taken destructive paths, but they are able to rationalize their choices, at least for a time. Then one day their cleverness catches up with them and they find themselves on the broad path that promised pleasure and plenty but delivered only pain.

Narrow is the gate and difficult is the way that leads to life, and there are few who find it. God gave Adam and Eve the ability to choose between the Tree of Life and the Tree of the Knowledge of Good and Evil. The Tree of Knowledge seems very appealing but its fruit is poison. The world spends itself in having intimate knowledge and relationship with good *and* evil, and the result is always destruction. Broad is the way.

Jesus invites us to partake of the Tree of Life. "Enter by the narrow gate," He says. In John 14:6, He spells it out: "I am the way, the truth, and the life. No one comes to the Father except through Me" (another verse the world does not care to quote—too restrictive for politically correct, multicultural diversity).

This little gate is so narrow that you cannot carry anything with you except total dependence upon God through faith in the Lord Jesus. But it is all you will ever need. In fact, without faith, you cannot enter at all. "For without faith it is impossible to please Him, for he who comes to God must believe that He is, and that He is a rewarder of those who diligently seek Him" (Hebrews 11:6). It is only through the gateway of faith that you will find Heaven on Earth.

Fruit Doesn't Lie

Beware of false prophets, who come to you in sheep's clothing, but inwardly they are ravenous wolves. You will know them by their fruits. Do men gather grapes from thornbushes or figs from thistles? Even so, every good tree bears good fruit, but a bad tree bears bad fruit. A good tree cannot bear bad fruit, nor can a bad tree bear good fruit. Every tree that does not bear good fruit is cut down and thrown into the fire. Therefore by their fruits you will know them. (Matthew 7:15-20)

Jesus told us to beware of false prophets. How do we recognize them? By their fruit.

- ❧ Every good tree bears good fruit.
- ❧ Every bad tree bears bad fruit.
- ❧ A good tree cannot bear bad fruit.
- ❧ A bad tree cannot bear good fruit.

Each tree brings forth what is in it. Fruit is the overflow of the life of the tree. If the fruit is bad, the tree is bad. If the tree is good, the fruit will be good.

What is the fruit of false prophets? The spirit of religion. False prophets always seek to lead us away from trusting in God. They want us to trust in them, in their gods, or in ourselves (our abilities, our strength, our understanding, our works, our behavior). These always lead to death.

False prophets offer us the fruit from The Tree of the Knowledge of Good and Evil. It may appear very pleasant, good for food and the way to life, but it alienates us from God and causes us to lean on our own understanding. Adam and Eve were deceived by the false prophet, the serpent in the Garden. They ate of this tree and disconnected from the life of God. Wisdom says,

Trust in the LORD with all your heart,
    And lean not on your own understanding;
In all your ways acknowledge Him,
    And He shall direct your paths.

(Proverbs 3:5-6)

When we set our hearts on the Lord and put all our trust in Him, He will direct our paths. We will be operating out of *His* wisdom and guidance. We will be tuned into life and dialed into prosperity. We will be eating from The Tree of Life, and will be able to discern the false prophets.

- *False prophets are false shepherds.* Though they come pretending to care for the sheep, they are actually wolves—thieves who break in to steal, kill and destroy. Jesus, the Good Shepherd, came to give us the abundant life of God (John 10:10).
- *False prophets come to sow tares in God's wheat fields.* The thing about tares is that they may look very much like wheat when they are young. But when they come into fruit, their true character is revealed—they are nothing but worthless weeds destined for destruction (Matthew 13:24-30).
- *False prophets load us up with rules and regulations (see Matthew 23:1-7).* They hit us with accusation, condemnation and rejection on the one hand, then they offer rationalization and self-justification on the other. It is all bad fruit from a bad tree.

God offers us good fruit from the good tree—the Tree of Life. It is the fruit of faith, trusting completely in God and not in ourselves. It is the fruit of forgiveness and acceptance through Jesus Christ. It is the fruit of intimate relationship with Him.

Fruit doesn't lie. False prophets will never bear good fruit; it will always have a poisonous seed within. Jesus Christ bears only good fruit;

it will always lead to abundant life with God. All those who know the Lord Jesus have the Holy Spirit dwelling within them. It is the work of the Spirit to bring forth the fruit of Jesus Christ in our lives: love, joy peace, longsuffering, kindness, goodness, faith, gentleness, and self-control (Galatians 5:22-23).

DOING THE WORKS OF GOD

Not everyone who says to Me, "Lord, Lord," shall enter the kingdom of heaven, but he who does the will of My Father in heaven. Many will say to Me, "Lord, Lord, have we not prophesied in Your name, cast out demons in Your name, and done many wonders in Your name?" And then I will declare to them, "I never knew you; depart from Me, you who practice lawlessness." (Matthew 7:21-23)

There are many false disciples who come to Jesus and say, "Lord, look at all we have done in Your name." They come presenting themselves to the Lord on the basis of their works and behavior. But they do not really know Him. In fact, Jesus declares, "I *never* knew you."

They also know nothing of the will of God. That is because they do not will to do His will and have no desire to fulfill His desire. They are into rules and regulations, not intimate relationship with the Father. They are entangled with the spirit of religion. They eat from the wrong tree. They suppose themselves to be doing good, but the good from that tree is as detrimental as the evil, for it leads them to trust in themselves and not in God. Though they claim to do wonders in His name, Jesus says they actually practice lawlessness.

Jesus said, "This is the work of God, that you believe in Him whom He sent" (John 6:29). Though these false prophets perform miracles in Jesus' name, they do not believe in Him, therefore they do not do the works of God. Nor are they pleasing to God because their faith is not in Him.

Performance-based religion will never please God because it is totally devoid of faith in Him. It is not good works and better behavior that is required but a new birth from above. Always and in everything, we must be completely dependent upon God. This is the will of our Father in heaven.

THE FOUNDATION OF HEAVEN ON EARTH

Therefore whoever hears these sayings of Mine, and does them, I will liken him to a wise man who built his house on the rock: and the rain descended, the floods came, and the winds blew and beat on that house; and it did not fall, for it was founded on the rock. But everyone who hears these sayings of Mine, and does not do them, will be like a foolish man who built his house on the sand: and the rain descended, the floods came, and the winds blew and beat on that house; and it fell. And great was its fall. (Matthew 7:24-27)

Jesus ends His sermon of Heaven on Earth with these words. They bear a striking similarity to statements made by rabbis in ancient Jewish commentaries. For instance, Adam Clarke offers these quotes in his commentary on this passage:

Rabbi Eleasar said, "The man whose knowledge exceeds his works, to whom is he like? He is like a tree which had many branches, and only a few roots; and, when the stormy winds came, it was plucked up and eradicated. But he whose good works are greater than his knowledge, to what is he like? He is like a tree which had few branches, and many roots; so that all the winds of heaven could not move it from its place." (*Pirke Aboth*)

Elisha, the son of Abuja, said, "The man who studies much in the law, and maintains good works, is like to a man who built a house, laying stones at the foundation, and building brick upon them; and, though many waters come against it, they cannot move it from its place. But the man who studies much in the law, and does not maintain good works, is like to a man who, in building his house, put brick at the foundation, and laid stones upon them, so that even gentle waters shall overthrow that house." (*Aboth Rab. Nath*)

These rabbis spoke very generally. Their words were good as far as they went but carried no weight of their own. They lacked authority and spoke no further than the current state of rabbinic interpretation would allow. Jesus, however, spoke with a specificity and sense of authority about His own words, "these sayings of *Mine.*" There was no dithering to His words. They simply carried great power. So great was the authority inherent in His teaching, the people were amazed.

> *And so it was, when Jesus had ended these sayings, that the people were astonished at His teaching, for He taught them as one having authority, and not as the scribes. (Matthew 7:28-29)*

The difference, then, between foolishness and wisdom, between shifting sand and a solid foundation, is as simple as the difference between hearing and doing *whatever Jesus says.* The kingdom of Heaven on Earth is *His* kingdom, and *He* is its rightful ruler.

It is only as we hear and do what Jesus says that we will find the stability of heaven manifested on earth. The difference may not be apparent at first. A house built on sand may look very much like a house built on rock—until the storms come and the floodwaters rise. Then the pressures of life reveal the stability of the foundation.

A life built on hypocrisy, pride, an unexamined heart, stinginess, a critical spirit, worry and fear, and trusting in anything other than God will buckle and fall. But a life established on the foundation of a pure and honest heart, undivided, free of vengeance, full of love and forgiveness, tuned to the heart of the Father and His priorities, and full of faith and godly discernment—all that Jesus taught—will be able to weather any storm. For the kingdom of Heaven on Earth is a kingdom of stability and strength.

THE NATURE OF
HEAVEN ON EARTH

Authority and Discipleship in the Kingdom

J esus demonstrated the authority of Heaven on Earth by healing sicknesses and casting out demons. When He calmed the wind and waves, He showed that even the natural elements were subject to His kingdom (Matthew 8:23-27). Interspersed with these miraculous accounts are calls to discipleship, by which this authority would be multiplied in all the world.

The coming of Heaven on Earth required much more than patching up the old way of doing things, the religious traditions that had gathered around the instruction God gave in the Old Testament. As Jesus said,

> No one puts a piece of unshrunk cloth on an old garment; for the patch pulls away from the garment, and the tear is made worse. Nor do they put new wine into old wineskins, or else the wineskins break, the wine is spilled, and the wineskins are ruined. But they put new wine into new wineskins, and both are preserved. (Matthew 9:16-17)

New garments and wineskins were required because the least in the kingdom of Heaven on Earth is greater than even the greatest of Old Testament saints (Matthew 11:11). This, of course, brought opposition from those who enjoyed positions of power and influence through the old traditions that had bound up the ancient faith. Such resistance, however, can never defeat the work God is doing in the world. His kingdom overcomes all others but cannot itself be divided.

Heaven on Earth is forcefully advancing, not by political cunning or physical violence, but by the message of the gospel. Those who have tenacious faith in the Lord Jesus are the ones who are laying hold of it and seeing it happen. Mere curiosity will gain nothing. It is only those who are serious in their commitment to Him who will walk in kingdom authority, prevail over the oppositions of satan and the religious spirit, and know the peace of Christ in this life.

THE ACCESSIBLE KINGDOM

When He had come down from the mountain, great multitudes followed Him. And behold, a leper came and worshiped Him, saying, "Lord, if You are willing, You can make me clean." Then Jesus put out His hand and touched him, saying, "I am willing; be cleansed." Immediately his leprosy was cleansed. (Matthew 8:1-3)

In the Sermon of Heaven on Earth, Jesus taught them to pray, "Your kingdom come. Your will be done on earth as it is in heaven." The kingdom of God is the will of God being done on earth just as it is being done in heaven. When Jesus came down from the mount, a leper came and said, "Lord, if You are willing, You can heal me." He had no doubt that Jesus had the power and authority to heal, but he wanted to know what was the will of God in the matter. Would cleansing him of leprosy demonstrate the will of God being done on earth as it is in heaven? This was the only time anyone asked Jesus if He was willing to heal, and He settled the question: "*I am willing*; be cleansed." And the man was healed of leprosy.

Jesus then went into Capernaum, where he met a Roman centurion who desired Him to heal his servant, who was at home, paralyzed. Jesus again demonstrated the willingness of heaven to be manifested on earth. "I *will* come and heal him," He said (Matthew 8:5-13).

Next, Jesus came to Peter's house, where Peter's mother-in-law was sick with fever. Jesus touched her hand and the fever left her (Matthew 8:14-15). That evening, people came to the house bringing many who were demonized and sick. Jesus cast out the demons and healed all who were sick (Matthew 8:16-17). It was the will of God being done on earth as it is in heaven.

A little while later, Jesus crossed the Sea of Galilee to the country of the Gergesenes, where He was met by two men who were violently demon-possessed, and He cast out the evil spirits (Matthew 8:28-34). Then He got back into the boat and came back across to His own town, where He healed a paralytic who was brought to Him by his friends. "Son, be of good cheer; your sins are forgiven you," He said. When some of the scribes fumed over this, thinking Jesus a blasphemer, He said,

> *Why do you think evil in your hearts? For which is easier to say, "Your sins are forgiven you," or to say, "Arise and walk"? But that you may know that the Son of Man has power on earth to forgive sins,—then He said to the paralytic "Arise, take up your bed and go to your house."*

The man got up, took his bed and went home. The crowds marveled and gave God glory, because Jesus showed it was the will of God in heaven to release His power on earth to heal sickness and forgive sins (Matthew 9:1-8).

Not long afterwards, a ruler in the synagogue asked Jesus to come home and lay His hand on his daughter so that she would live. Jesus was willing, so He got up and followed him. Along the way, a woman who suffered from constant bleeding came up behind Jesus to touch the hem of His garment. "Be of good cheer, daughter, your faith has made you well," He told her, and the woman was healed. Jesus was completely willing for her to receive it. Arriving at the house of the synagogue ruler, Jesus went in and raised the dead girl to life, for it is the will of God in heaven that even the dead be restored on earth (Matthew 9:18-26).

When Jesus left there, two blind men began to follow Him, crying out, "Son of David, have mercy on us." Jesus stopped and said, "Do you believe that I am able to do this?" They answered, "Yes, Lord." He touched their eyes and said, "According to your faith let it be to you." They believed that He was both able and willing to grant their request, and they received their sight (Matthew 9:27-31).

Then a man was brought to Him who was mute and demonized. Jesus cast out the demon and the man was able to speak. The crowds were amazed. "It was never seen like this in Israel." But the Pharisees had no understanding of the will of God in heaven. They answered, "He casts out demons by the ruler of the demons" (Matthew 9:32-34).

Jesus did not turn away anyone who came to Him in faith but granted them whatever they were seeking. For the kingdom of Heaven on Earth is the willingness of God to forgive sins, heal diseases and set the captives free.

THE KINGDOM RECEIVED BY FAITH

Now when Jesus had entered Capernaum, a centurion came to Him, pleading with Him, saying, "Lord, my servant is lying at home paralyzed, dreadfully tormented."

And Jesus said to him, "I will come and heal him."

The centurion answered and said, "Lord, I am not worthy that You should come under my roof. But only speak a word, and my servant will be healed. For I also am a man under authority, having soldiers under me. And I say to this one, 'Go,' and he goes; and to another, 'Come,' and he comes; and to my servant, 'Do this,' and he does it."

When Jesus heard it, He marveled, and said to those who followed, "Assuredly, I say to you, I have not found such great faith, not even in Israel! And I say to you that many will come from east and west, and sit down with Abraham, Isaac, and Jacob in the kingdom of heaven. But the sons of the kingdom will be cast out into outer darkness. There will be weeping and gnashing of teeth."

Then Jesus said to the centurion, "Go your way; and as you have believed, so let it be done for you." And his servant was healed that same hour. (Matthew 8:5-13)

This account of Jesus healing the centurion's servant has many things to teach us, about healing, authority and the dynamics of faith. But it also has something very important to teach us about the kingdom of Heaven on Earth.

First, notice that this man who came to Jesus was a Roman soldier. In fact, he was a commander over many Roman soldiers. In other words, he was not of Israel, not of those who were given promise of the divine kingdom. However, he was a man who recognized and understood authority. More than that, he was a man who understood faith, and he put his faith in Jesus. In fact, Jesus described it as "great faith," greater than any He had found in Israel. Here is a very remarkable thing: though this man was not of Israel, he had greater faith than those who *were* of Israel.

That leads to the second important point. After commending this Roman centurion for his great faith, Jesus immediately uses it to make a powerful declaration about the kingdom of heaven: "And I say to you that many will come from east and west, and sit down with Abraham, Isaac, and Jacob in the kingdom of heaven." The kingdom of heaven will include those who will come from the east and west, that is, those who are not of Israel. They will "sit down" (the Greek word means to recline at table, as at a banquet) with Abraham, Isaac and Jacob. In other words, they will have an equal share in the kingdom.

Then Jesus adds this surprising statement: "But the sons of the kingdom will be cast out into outer darkness. There will be weeping and gnashing of teeth." The "sons of the kingdom" refers to those who by natural birth belong to those to whom the kingdom was promised. However, when the promise is not received by faith it has no power. As the author of Hebrews notes concerning those Israelites who were delivered in the Exodus, but later died in the wilderness instead of entering into the Promised Land, "So we see that they could not enter in because of unbelief ... For indeed the gospel was preached to us as well as to them; but the word which they heard did not profit them, not being mixed with faith in those who heard it" (Hebrews 3:19; 4:2).

The "sons of the kingdom" thought that the kingdom of heaven automatically belonged to them because of who they were, that they were of Israel. But the surprising turnabout is that, although many non-Israelites will enter into the kingdom, there will also be Israelites who will be cast out.

The difference is all about faith. Those who, like the Roman centurion, recognize the authority of King Jesus and believe in Him, regardless of their ethnicity, will be received into full fellowship in His kingdom. Those who do not believe, who reject the King, will have no place in His kingdom. For the kingdom of Heaven on Earth is not received by rights of natural birth, but by faith.

Following the King

And when Jesus saw great multitudes about Him, He gave a command to depart to the other side. Then a certain scribe came and said to Him, "Teacher, I will follow You wherever You go." And Jesus said to him, "Foxes have holes and birds of the air have nests, but the Son of Man has nowhere to lay His head."

Then another of His disciples said to Him, "Lord, let me first go and bury my father." But Jesus said to him, "Follow Me, and let the dead bury their own dead." (Matthew 8:18-22)

As Jesus passed on from there, He saw a man named Matthew sitting at the tax office. And He said to him "Follow Me." So he arose and followed Him. (Matthew 9:9)

What does it mean to follow the King? Matthew gives us three vignettes. The first is about a scribe, a teacher of the Law who was quite taken with Jesus and His message. He said, "Teacher, I will follow You wherever you go." There is no reason to doubt that he meant it, at least as much as he understood it. But did he really know what he was asking? Jesus laid it out for him: "The Son of Man has nowhere to lay His head." He was not speaking of a life of poverty, but a life lived on a different basis. Follow Jesus and there is no telling where you might end up. Where He was heading, there would also be lot of persecution for Him and his disciples to endure (see Matthew 10:16-26). To follow Jesus is to step away from the security offered by the world and live in full dependence on Him.

The second brief story is about "another of His disciples," which would indicate that the scribe of the first story really was also a disciple of Jesus, at least at some level. This second disciple wanted to follow Jesus but first desired to go and bury his father. If he was the oldest son, it would have been his responsibility to do so. Since he was out in public, he was no longer in the private mourning period, which indicates that his father's body had already been placed in the tomb. But it was the custom of Jews back then to go back a year later to gather up the bones and place them in a special stone box called an ossuary. That is likely what this man is referring to.

However, in practical terms, "Let me bury my father," meant, "Lord, I can't follow you this year. Let me wait until next year." Jesus answered, "Follow me, and let the dead bury their own dead." He was not speaking against the burial custom or the young man's sense of responsibility to honor his father. He was directing the man to the proper perspective. Had not the young man heard Him preach earlier, "Seek first the kingdom of God and His righteousness, and all these things shall be added to you"? That set the priority concerning everything, even family matters. "Follow Me," Jesus said, and everything else that is needed will be properly tended. "Let the dead bury their own dead." The man's father would be reburied by those who stayed behind. It was a secondary matter, as are all things when the King has come. The main thing is to follow the King.

A little later, Matthew tells of another call to follow Jesus—his own. Matthew was a tax collector, probably a customs agent, working for the Herodian system that was much despised by the Jewish people. He was sitting at his booth one day when Jesus came and said, "Follow Me." We do not know how the first two men responded, whether or not they followed Jesus with a deeper understanding and commitment, but we do know about Matthew: "So he arose and followed Him." We do not know the issues of his heart that brought him to his decision, but he decided to leave behind the security of his position and make the kingdom of God his priority.

Matthew then threw a party for Jesus and His disciples (Luke 5:29 tells us this was at Matthew's house), and many of his own friends and fellow tax collectors came, too. The Pharisees were once again offended. "Why does your Teacher eat with tax collectors and sinners?" Though they were neither bold enough nor polite enough to ask Him directly, Jesus heard their remarks and said, "Those who are well have no need of a physician, but those who are sick. But go and learn what this means: 'I desire mercy and not sacrifice.' For I did not come to call the righteous, but sinners, to repentance" (Matthew 9:12-13).

The kingdom of Heaven on Earth is not for those who deem themselves righteous but for those who recognize their need of repentance. The repentance required is not only about turning away from the works of darkness but also turning from the dead works of religion (sacrifice without mercy) to the "physician" of souls.

To follow the King we must recognize our need of Him, give up the security of the world and depend on Him alone, and make His kingdom our priority. Those who do will find Heaven on Earth.

Signs of the Kingdom

Then Jesus went about all the cities and villages, teaching in their synagogues, preaching the gospel of the kingdom, and healing every sickness and every disease among the people. (Matthew 9:35)

The ministry of the Lord Jesus Christ was to preach the "gospel of the kingdom," the good news that the kingdom of heaven was now present on earth. He not only preached this, He also demonstrated it by healing every sickness and disease that was brought before Him.

The kingdom of God had begun breaking into the world but Jesus now greatly desired to accelerate it:

> *But when He saw the multitudes, He was moved with compassion for them, because they were weary and scattered, like sheep having no shepherd. Then He said to His disciples, "The harvest truly is plentiful, but the laborers are few. Therefore pray the Lord of the harvest to send out laborers into His harvest." (Matthew 9:36-38)*

The kingdom of Heaven on Earth is a kingdom of harvest. In the very next verse we see the Lord of the Harvest sending forth His laborers to do exactly what He Himself had been doing:

> *And when He had called His twelve disciples to Him, He gave them power over unclean spirits, to cast them out, and to heal all kinds of sickness and all kinds of disease ... These twelve Jesus sent out and commanded them, saying: "Do not go into the way of the Gentiles, and do not enter a city of the Samaritans. But go rather to the lost sheep of the house of Israel. And as you go, preach, saying, 'The kingdom of heaven is at hand.' Heal the sick, cleanse the lepers, raise the dead, cast out demons. Freely you have received, freely give." (Matthew 10:1, 5-8)*

Just as Jesus went about announcing the kingdom of Heaven on Earth and displaying the signs of the kingdom, He chose His disciples and sent them out to do the same. He gave them power and authority to expel demonic spirits, heal all kinds of sickness and disease, even to raise the dead.

When John the Baptist heard about the works of Christ being done, he sent two of his disciples to ask, "Are You the Coming One, or do we look for another?"

> *Jesus answered and said to them, "Go and tell John the things which you hear and see: The blind see and the lame walk; the lepers are cleansed*

and the deaf hear; the dead are raised up and the poor have the gospel
preached to them. And blessed is he who is not offended because of Me."
(Matthew 11:4-6)

Life, wholeness and freedom are the signs that the kingdom of heaven
truly is present on earth. The Lord Jesus gives power and authority to *all*
His disciples to bring forth these signs and gather in the harvest. They
have all been performed many times over in the history of the Church
and are coming forth with even greater frequency today.

The Kingdom That Divides

Now whatever city or town you enter, inquire who in it is worthy, and
stay there till you go out. And when you go into a household, greet it. If the
household is worthy, let your peace come upon it. But if it is not worthy,
let your peace return to you. And whoever will not receive you nor hear
your words, when you depart from that house or city, shake off the dust
from your feet. (Matthew 10:11-14)

Jesus sent the disciples out to preach the kingdom and manifest it
through signs but He cautioned them that not everyone would receive
it. There would be persecution ahead. Some would be hospitable to them
and believe their message; others would reject it. Those who received
would have a blessing of peace given to them. For those who turned away
the message, and the messengers, there was no blessing to offer. We will
see Jesus talk about this again in Matthew 25:31-45, where He speaks
of the division of the sheep and the goats based on how they receive His
disciples. The principle, implied here but much more explicit there, is
found in Matthew 25:40, "Inasmuch as you did it to one of the least of
these my brethren, you did it to Me."

"Behold, I send you out as sheep in the midst of wolves," Jesus said,
"Therefore, be wise as serpents and harmless as doves" (Matthew 10:16).
They would need to have great prudence and be innocent of evil. He

warned them that they would be brought up and accused before Jewish councils and flogged in the synagogues (v. 17). They would be betrayed to Gentile governors and kings but the Holy Spirit would show them what to say (vv. 18-20). They would be widely hated in Israel because of Jesus' name, and persecuted from city to city for being His disciples. Just as their Master would be despised, so they would be, too. It would be a comfort to be in such good company as His (vv. 21-25).

"Therefore do not fear them. For there is nothing covered that will not be revealed, and hidden that will not be known" (v. 26). The true nature of things would be made manifest and what was now being revealed to them in secret, they would soon preach abroad (v. 27). Though men may put to death the body, they cannot touch the soul (v. 28), for the God who takes care of the sparrows, which are of very little value in the marketplace, knows the number of hairs on our heads, because we are of far greater value to Him (vv. 29-31).

"Therefore whoever confesses Me before men, him I will also confess before My Father who is in heaven. But whoever denies Me before men, him I will also deny before My Father who is in heaven" (vv. 32-33). Here is the great dividing line: Whoever believes and confesses the gospel of Jesus Christ openly on earth will be acknowledged before God in heaven by the Lord Jesus. Whoever rejects Him on earth will be denied by Him in heaven. It is a sobering judgment, a sword that will even separate family members from one another. But if one chooses Jesus as King, he must love Him even more than father, mother, daughter and son (vv. 34-37). It is not that these relationships are to be devalued but that our relationship with Christ is to be honored above all.

All these things awaited the disciples as they fulfilled this great commission, and came to pass within a generation after Jesus went to the Cross. His cross becomes one each of us must bear (v. 38). It is the cost of following Jesus (was the scribe who promised to follow Him everywhere really ready for this?). It is the difference between losing life and finding it. "He who finds his life will lose it, and he who loses his life for My sake will find it" (v. 39).

Now Jesus returned again to the reward for those who receive the ministry of the disciples:

He who receives you receives Me, and he who receives Me receives Him who sent Me. He who receives a prophet in the name of a prophet shall receive a prophet's reward. And he who receives a righteous man in the name of a righteous man shall receive a righteous man's reward. And whoever gives one of these little ones only a cup of cold water in the name of a disciple, assuredly, I say to you, he shall by no means lose his reward. (Matthew 10:40-42)

The kingdom of Heaven on Earth is a reward for those who believe the message of the gospel brought by the disciples. The cost for confessing the Lord Jesus may be great but the cost for rejecting Him is infinitely greater.

THE KINGDOM THAT MAKES ONE GREAT

Assuredly, I say to you, among those born of women there has not risen one greater than John the Baptist; but he who is least in the kingdom of heaven is greater than he. (Matthew 11:11)

The Old Testament is full of many mighty men of God who accomplished great and powerful things, but none of them was greater than John the Baptist. He was more than a prophet—he was a forerunner. Jesus identifies him as the one of whom Malachi spoke: "Behold, I send my messenger before Your face, who will prepare Your way before You" (Matthew 11:10, quoting Malachi 3:1).

The expectation of Malachi was that God would once again send the prophet Elijah. "Behold, I will send you Elijah the prophet before the coming of the great and terrible day of the LORD" (Malachi 4:5). Jesus said, "All the prophets and the law prophesied until John. And if you are willing to receive it, he is Elijah who is to come" (Matthew 11:13-14).

However, as great as John was, Jesus said, "He who is least in the kingdom of heaven is greater than he." Follow the logic and it leads to an amazing conclusion:

- ⮞ John the Baptist was greater than all of the Old Testament saints.
- ⮞ The least one in the kingdom of heaven is greater than John the Baptist.
- ⮞ Therefore, the least one in the kingdom of heaven is greater than all of the Old Testament saints.

Now, this does not mean that the least in the kingdom are any greater in holiness, devotion or faith. Rather, it has to do with the greatness of the kingdom of heaven itself. The prophets of old only foresaw it but saints of the kingdom are actually a part of it. Of these great Old Testament heroes, the author of Hebrews writes,

> *These all died in faith, not having received the promises, but having seen them afar off were assured of them, embraced them and confessed that they were strangers and pilgrims on the earth ...*
>
> *And all these, having obtained a good testimony through faith, did not receive the promise, God having provided something better for us, that they should not be perfect apart from us. (Hebrews 11:13, 39-40)*

They obtained a good testimony because of their great faith, even though they did not live to see the day for which they believed. However, God has provided something for us that is even better, which builds on their ancient witness and is indeed a fulfillment of it—the kingdom of Heaven on Earth.

- ⮞ It is the kingdom of the *New* Covenant, which is based on better promises (Hebrews 8:6) and instituted in the blood of the Lord Jesus Christ (Luke 22:20).

- ↝ It is the kingdom of righteousness, peace and joy in the Holy Spirit (Romans 14:17). The Spirit of God only rested *on* the heroes of the Old Testament, and only on a few. In the New Covenant God has given His Spirit to dwell *in* every member as well as *on* them.

- ↝ It is the kingdom of the *greater works of Jesus.* Jesus said, "Most assuredly, I say to you, he who believes in Me, the works that I do he will do also; and greater works than these he will do, because I go to My Father. And whatever you ask in My name, that I will do, that the Father may be glorified in the Son" (John 14:12-13)

The kingdom of Heaven on Earth is a kingdom of greatness and confers greatness on all who belong to it.

THE KINGDOM FORCEFULLY ADVANCING

And from the days of John the Baptist until now the kingdom of heaven suffers violence, and the violent take it by force. (Matthew 11:12)

From the days of John the Baptist until now, the kingdom of heaven has been forcefully advancing, and forceful men lay hold of it. (NIV)

The law and the prophets were until John. Since that time the kingdom of God has been preached, and everyone is pressing into it. (Luke 16:16)

Do not be put off by the language of violence and force, for Paul tells us there is a spiritual warfare going on. He tells us to "put on the full armor of God," which includes the "sword of the Spirit, which is the Word of God" (Ephesians 6:11-17). "For we do not wrestle against flesh and blood, but against principalities, against powers, against the rulers of the darkness of this age, against spiritual hosts of wickedness in the heavenly places" (v. 12).

The Gospel of Matthew does not paint John as a passive and gentle preacher but as an aggressive, thundering prophet, castigating unbelieving Pharisees and Sadducees:

Brood of vipers! Who warned you to flee from the wrath to come? Therefore bear fruits worthy of repentance, and do not think to say to yourselves, "We have Abraham as our father." For I say to you that God is able to raise up children to Abraham from these stones. And even now the ax is laid to the root of the trees. Therefore every tree which does not bear good fruit is cut down and thrown into the fire. (Matthew 3:7-10)

Jesus asked concerning John, "What did you go out into the wilderness to see? A reed shaken by the wind? But what did you go out to see? A man clothed in soft garments? Indeed, those who wear soft clothing are in kings' houses. But what did you go out to see? A prophet? Yes, I say to you, and more than a prophet" (Matthew 11:7-9). John came on the scene with a powerful intensity that shook the world from the epicenter of the Judean desert. "From the days of John the Baptist until now, the kingdom of heaven has been forcefully advancing."

Notice the words, "pressing," "suffers violence" and "forcefully advancing." The Greek verb for all three is *biazo*, which speaks of the use of force. In Matthew 11:12, the form of *biazo* used is *biazetai* and is either in the passive or middle voice. The passive rendering is "suffers violence." The middle voice is as the *NIV* has it, "forcefully advancing."

Luke records the same saying as Matthew. In Luke's version, "The kingdom of God has been preached" correlates with "suffers violence" or "has been forcefully advancing." "Forcefully advancing" seems to be a better parallel to "has been preached" than does "suffers violence." We do not normally think of the kingdom of God being preached as something that it suffers, but as an advance.

In the latter part of Luke 16:16, "everyone is pressing into it" relates to "the violent take it by force," or "forceful men lay hold of it." Here the Greek verb *biazetai*, in the middle voice, means to "crowd oneself into." That is exactly what the kingdom of heaven has been doing since the time of John the Baptist—it has been "crowding itself" (*biazetai*) into the world, forcefully advancing through the preaching of the gospel. In response, forceful men have been laying hold of it—they have been "pressing into it" or "crowding themselves" (*biazetai*) into it.

Some have supposed that the "violent men" are wicked men who seek to overturn the kingdom. Notice, though, that Jesus did not say that violent, forceful men *try* to take it by force. They actually *do* take it by force. But how is it possible that the kingdom of God can be overcome by wicked men, when Jesus said of His Church that the gates of hell would not prevail against it (Matthew 16:18)? The answer is that it cannot. Remember also what John said, that greater is He that is in us than he that is in the world (1 John 4:4).

No, the wicked do not and cannot take the kingdom of God by force. Rather, Jesus is talking about men responding to the gospel of the kingdom by faith, pressing into the kingdom, just as the kingdom is pressing into the world. Matthew 11:12 and Luke 16:16 refer to the same thing.

The kingdom of God advances in many ways. By the preaching of the gospel. By healings and deliverances. By signs, wonders and miracles in the power of the Holy Spirit. By prayer, as we pray the way Jesus taught us to pray: "Kingdom of God, *keep on coming*" (that is the sense of the Greek text in Matthew 6:10).

The kingdom of God is pressing itself into the world, and forceful men are taking hold of it. It is like Jacob wrestling with the angel of the LORD: "I will not let You go until You bless me" (Genesis 32:26). Or like the man who stumbled upon a rich treasure in a field, then went out and sold all that he had so he could buy that field and possess that treasure. It is seeking first the kingdom of God and letting God take care of everything else. It is asking until you receive, seeking until you find and knocking until the door is opened unto you. It is a bulldog tenacity. In a word, it is the force of faith, believing what God has said. Without faith, it is impossible to please God, but with faith, all things are possible (Mark 9:23).

Ever since the days of John the Baptist, the kingdom of God has been powerfully breaking into the world and men of tenacious faith have been laying hold of it. When we are fully focused on God's kingdom, we will see it manifest in very powerful ways, but if we treat it casually, we will hardly recognize it.

The kingdom of Heaven on Earth is forcefully advancing and we lay hold of it by the force of faith, believing the Word of God and the message of the gospel.

The Kingdom Hidden and Revealed

At that time Jesus answered and said, "I thank You, Father, Lord of heaven and earth, that You have hidden these things from the wise and prudent and have revealed them to babes. Even so, Father, for so it seemed good in Your sight." (Matthew 11:25-26)

Jesus rebuked the Jewish leaders of His generation for their fickleness. They were like little children who could not be pleased. They did not like the happy games; they did play the sad. They did not rejoice with the dance; they did not mourn with the dirge (Matthew 11:16-17).

For John came neither eating nor drinking, and they say, "He has a demon." The Son of Man came eating and drinking, and they say, "Look, a glutton and a winebibber, a friend of tax collectors and sinners!" But wisdom is justified by her children. (Matthew 11:18-19)

They rejected both the repentance preached by John and the good news of the kingdom proclaimed by Jesus. God offers no other alternative; only this one brings eternal life. That was foolishness to the religious rulers, but the wisdom of God would soon reveal who were truly His children.

Jesus began to denounce the Jewish cities where He had performed so many miracles but which had refused to repent, persisting in unbelief.

If the signs and wonders He had done in Chorazin, Bethsaida and Capernaum had been performed in Tyre and Sidon, or even in Sodom and Gomorrah, they would have repented long ago and would not have been destroyed. But now Israel would face a day of judgment that was much more severe than any suffered by those Old Testament cities (Matthew 11:20-24). This terrible verdict was fulfilled with the siege of Jerusalem and the ferocious destruction of the Temple in AD 70.

Then Jesus "answered" the matter. That is, He drew His conclusion, offering a prayer of thanksgiving to the Father. "I thank You, Father, Lord of heaven and earth, that You have hidden these things from the wise and prudent and have revealed them to babes. Even so, Father, for so it seemed good in Your sight."

God has revealed to babes things He has hidden from those who consider themselves wise and learned in this world. There is a wisdom that is of the world, but it is not like the wisdom of heaven.

> *Who is wise and understanding among you? Let him show by good conduct that his works are done in the meekness of wisdom. But if you have bitter envy and self-seeking in your hearts, do not boast and lie against the truth. This wisdom does not descend from above, but is earthly, sensual, demonic. For where envy and self-seeking exist, confusion and every evil thing are there.*
>
> *But the wisdom that is from above is first pure, then peaceable, gentle, willing to yield, full of mercy and good fruits, without partiality and without hypocrisy. Now the fruit of righteousness is sown in peace by those who make peace. (James 3:13-18)*

The wisdom that is from above is the wisdom of Heaven on Earth and reveals the righteousness and peace of the Father's kingdom. God does not withhold it; He is willing to share it with all who are willing to receive. But the world has received an earthbound wisdom that is limited to the senses, demonic in nature and brings forth evil and confusion. Therefore the wise of this world are unable to embrace the wisdom that is from above. So God reveals it to the babes, the simple, the weak—those whom the world considers foolish.

> *Because the foolishness of God is wiser than men, and the weakness of God is stronger than men. For you see your calling, brethren, that not many wise according to the flesh, not many mighty, not many noble, are called. But God has chosen the foolish things of the world to put to shame the wise, and God has chosen the weak things of the world to put to shame the things which are mighty; and the base things of the world and the things which are despised God has chosen, and the things which are not, to bring to nothing the things that are, that no flesh should glory in His presence. But of Him you are in Christ Jesus, who became for us wisdom from God. (1 Corinthians 1:25-30)*

Jesus *is* the wisdom from above, the wisdom God greatly desires for us to have. He bypasses the wisdom of the world and reveals the Father to all who receive Him.

> *All things have been delivered to Me by My Father, and no one knows the Son except the Father. Nor does anyone know the Father except the Son, and the one to whom the Son wills to reveal Him. (Matthew 11:27-28)*

The wisdom of Heaven on Earth is the revelation of the Father in Jesus Christ the Son. We find an example of this a few chapters later, where Jesus asks His disciples who they say He is. Peter answers, "You are the Christ, the Son of the Living God," to which Jesus responded, "Blessed are you, Simon Bar-Jonah, for flesh and blood has not revealed this to you, but My Father in heaven" (Matthew 16:16-17). This wisdom comes only by divine revelation, but Jesus now offers it to all who will take hold of it and welcome the peace with God that is found in Him.

The kingdom of Heaven on Earth, though rejected by the wisdom of the world, is revealed to those who are willing to receive its king, Jesus Christ, who is made for us the wisdom of God.

The Kingdom of Sabbath Rest

Come to Me, all you who labor and are heavy laden, and I will give you rest. Take My yoke upon you and learn from Me, for I am gentle and lowly in heart, and you will find rest for your souls. For My yoke is easy and My burden is light. (Matthew 11:28-30).

For the Son of Man is Lord even of the Sabbath. (Matthew 12:8)

Early Jewish tradition spoke about taking on the "yoke" of the Law of Moses. However, this was a hard yoke that no one was able to bear. In the early Church, when a group of legalistic Jewish believers wanted to impose the Law on Gentile Christians, Peter rose up at the Jerusalem council and said, "Now therefore, why do you test God by putting a yoke on the neck of the disciples which neither our fathers nor we were able to bear?" (Acts 15:10). In Romans 7, Paul details his own desperate struggle—and ultimate failure—to bear this bondage and uphold the Law, finally finding deliverance in Jesus Christ (v. 25). The centerpiece of his letter to the Galatians is found in 5:1, "Stand fast therefore in the liberty by which Christ has made us free, and do not be entangled again with a yoke of bondage."

Jesus calls us to a different yoke. Not the yoke of Moses, which He came to fulfill (Matthew 5:17), but His own. To take His yoke means that we must set aside all other yokes. Formerly, the Law was a "tutor" whose purpose was to bring us to Christ (Galatians 3:24). Now that He has come, we take *His* yoke and learn of *Him*. The yoke of the Law was heavy and difficult; the yoke of Jesus is easy and light. It is a yoke of freedom, not of bondage, and the promise of Jesus is that by taking His yoke, we will find rest for our souls.

The rest we find in the Lord Jesus Christ is the fulfillment of the Law and the Sabbath rest it required. The Sabbath was a type; Jesus is the full realization to which the Sabbath could only point. Indeed, Jesus called Himself the "Lord of the Sabbath."

One day, as Jesus was walking through a field of grain, His disciples helped themselves to a little bit of it and ate. This was on a Sabbath. A group of Pharisees witnessed this and were upset. Not because of *what* they did, which was quite acceptable by Law and custom, but by *when* they did it. They complained to Jesus, "Look, Your disciples are doing what is not lawful to do on the Sabbath." But Jesus said to them:

> *Have you not read what David did when he was hungry, he and those who were with him: how he entered the house of God and ate the showbread which was not lawful for him to eat, nor for those who were with him, but only for the priests? Or have you not read in the law that on the Sabbath the priests in the temple profane the Sabbath, and are blameless? Yet I say to you that in this place there is One greater than the temple. But if you had known what this means, "I desire mercy and not sacrifice," you would not have condemned the guiltless. For the Son of Man is Lord even of the Sabbath. (Matthew 12:3-8)*

Jesus vindicated the act of His disciples by comparing it with three examples from the Law and the Prophets:

- ❧ It was not lawful for David to eat the sacred bread, which was a special offering to the Lord to be eaten only by the priests. Yet the necessity of hunger prevailed. How much more would this be true of Jesus, who was recognized with the messianic title Son of David (Matthew 9:27; 12:23; 15:22; 20:30-31; 21:9)? He accepted this designation, and even argued later that, not only was He the Son of David but He was also greater than David was because He was David's Lord (Matthew 22:41-46).
- ❧ It was not lawful to work on the Sabbath, and yet the priests of the Lord did not refrain from their work on that holy day. If the service of the Temple was exempt, then how much more would this be true of Jesus, who was greater than the

Temple? On another occasion, He even compared His body to the Temple: "Destroy this temple and in three days I will raise it up" (John 2:18-22).

    ও God desires mercy more than sacrifice. That is what the Lord said by the prophet Hosea: "For I desire mercy and not sacrifice, and the knowledge of God more than burnt offerings" (Hosea 6:6). There is a principle that is greater than the requirement of the Law and that is the mercy of God.

As if the Pharisees were not already scandalized enough by what Jesus said, He concluded with this declaration: "For the Son of Man is Lord even of the Sabbath." Here was another designation with messianic implication, for "Son of Man" spoke explicitly of His humanity but also implied His divinity (see Daniel 7:13-14). As Messiah and Lord, Jesus was greater than the Sabbath.

Jesus then went into their synagogue where, seeing a man who had a withered hand, the Pharisees asked, "Is it lawful to heal on the Sabbath?" (Matthew 12:10) They were still looking for a way to entrap Him. Turning the table on them, Jesus asked, "What man is there among you who has one sheep, and if it falls into a pit on the Sabbath, will not lay hold of it and lift it out?" (v. 11).

No one answered; it was an accepted practice to rescue one's livestock, even on the Sabbath. Then Jesus answered them, while at the same time revealing the hypocrisy of their question, "Of how much more value then is a man than a sheep? Therefore it is lawful to do good on the Sabbath" (v. 12). Then to prove the point, He said to the man, "Stretch out your hand." The man stretched out his hand and it was healed (v. 13). The Pharisees were livid, and went out plotting how they might destroy Jesus.

Jesus is the fulfillment of the Sabbath, the Temple, the Law of Moses and the promise God made to David. He calls us to set aside all other yokes and take up His, for it is easy and His burden is light, and we shall find rest for our souls. For the kingdom of Heaven on Earth is a kingdom of Sabbath rest.

The Kingdom of Quiet Revolution

But when Jesus knew it, He withdrew from there. And great multitudes
followed Him, and He healed them all. Yet He warned them not to make
Him known. (Matthew 12:15-16)

Jesus had so angered the Pharisees with His claim to be Lord over the
Sabbath, they went out scheming how they might bring Him down.
When Jesus learned of this, He departed. His kingdom is forceful,
and those who enter in are passionate for it, but it is not about violent
physical conflict.

As He left, large crowds followed after Him, many of whom were
sick, for Jesus had just demonstrated that healing is a good thing and it
is the Father's will to heal even on the Sabbath. They came because they
believed. Matthew notes the result very simply: "He healed them all."

After healing the multitude, Jesus strictly admonished them not to
make it widely known. He wanted to avoid the additional publicity, perhaps because He did not wish to exacerbate the situation of the Pharisees
and confirm them in their hardness of heart, for there were still some among
them who were open to His message. But there was an even greater reason.
Matthew sees in His reticence a fulfillment of what Isaiah foretold:

Behold! My Servant whom I have chosen,
 My Beloved in whom My soul is well pleased!
I will put My Spirit upon Him,
 And He will declare justice to the Gentiles.
He will not quarrel nor cry out,
 Nor will anyone hear His voice in the streets.
A bruised reed He will not break,
 And smoking flax He will not quench,
Till He sends forth justice to victory;
 And in His name Gentiles will trust.
 (Matthew 12:18-31, quoting Isaiah 42:1-4)

Though this passage may also have had a reference to Israel, the Servant whom God chose, in whom He was well pleased and upon whom He put His Spirit, is the Lord Jesus (see Matthew 3:16-17). He was not a political agitator. He did not come as a rabble-rouser or one who stirred up treason. He did not get into shouting matches. He did not treat harshly those who were brokenhearted or fading into despair, the "bruised reeds" and "smoking flaxes." He came for a larger purpose: to declare justice and set things right, not just for Israel, but for all the nations. He not only declared justice, He has been bringing it forth, and His cause shall be victorious.

His conquest does not come by military combat or political maneuverings, but by the preaching of the gospel. Before He ascended to heaven, He declared that all authority in heaven and earth had been given to Him. Then He commissioned His disciples to go and "make disciples of all the nations" (Matthew 28:18-19). This commission will not fail but will be fulfilled, and justice shall come to all the nations through the proclamation of the good news of Jesus Christ.

THE UNDIVIDED KINGDOM

Every kingdom divided against itself is brought to desolation, and every city or house divided against itself will not stand. If Satan casts out Satan, he is divided against himself. How then will his kingdom stand? And if I cast out demons by Beelzebub, by whom do your sons cast them out? Therefore they shall be your judges. But if I cast out demons by the Spirit of God, surely the kingdom of God has come upon you. (Matthew 12:25-28)

Jesus healed a man who was demon-possessed, blind and mute. He cast out the demon so that the man could see and speak (Matthew 12: 22-23). When some of the Pharisees heard of this, they came and accused Jesus of casting out demons by *Beelzebub* (literally, "Lord of the Flies") whom they considered the ruler over demons (v. 24).

Now, if it had been just one or two demons that Jesus expelled, they might have been able to make a good argument that satan was causing a few demons to retreat in order to gain some sort of strategic advantage. After all, satan is a schemer. But this was far more than a few. Jesus was casting out demons from the multitudes that followed, doing wholesale damage to the kingdom of satan and running roughshod over all his works. Indeed, this was one of the reasons He came, to destroy the works of the devil (Hebrews 2:14; 1 John 3:8).

Jesus answered their charge with a spiritual logic that turned the table on them. First, He pointed out that a kingdom or house divided against itself cannot stand. That being so, He then asked, if satan drives out satan, how can the kingdom of satan possibly stand. The Pharisees' accusation was logically incoherent—it made no sense.

Second, if Jesus was casting out demons by the power of Beelzebub, then by whose power did their "sons," their own exorcists, manage to cast out the few demons they were able to expel? The Pharisees were being hypocritical, which Jesus emphasized by adding, "Therefore they [the "sons"] will be your judges."

Third, if Jesus cast out demons by the Spirit and power of God (as indeed He did), then it was a sign that the kingdom of God had come into the world, for the Jews believed that when Messiah came, satan would be bound. Now here it was happening before their eyes, but in addition to the Pharisees being incoherent and hypocritical, they were also faithless.

Jesus was casting out demons everywhere He went, and He did it by the Spirit of God, as Peter later proclaimed: "God anointed Jesus of Nazareth with the Holy Spirit and with power, who went about doing good and healing all who were oppressed by the devil, for God was with Him" (Acts 10:38). This was not only a demonstration that the kingdom of God had now come but also that Jesus was indeed the Messiah.

The kingdom of God is an undivided kingdom. Though it would be a losing strategy for satan to divide his own kingdom, as Jesus pointed out, the kingdom of God not only has the power to divide it but was doing just that. Jesus added, "Or how can one enter a strong man's house and plunder his goods, unless he first binds the strong man? And then he will plunder his house" (Matthew 12:29).

By the Spirit of God, Jesus had come into the "house" of the "strong man," and binding him, was able to "plunder his goods," that is, to destroy the works of the devil and loose his captives. In this way, Jesus divided the kingdom of satan.

Having answered their charge, Jesus then addressed the Pharisees with sobering words about the indivisible nature of the kingdom of God:

> He who is not with Me is against Me, and he who does not gather with Me scatters abroad. Therefore I say to you, every sin and blasphemy will be forgiven men, but the blasphemy against the Spirit will not be forgiven men. Anyone who speaks a word against the Son of Man, it will be forgiven him; but whoever speaks against the Holy Spirit, it will not be forgiven him, either in this age or in the age to come. (Matthew 12:30-32)

The implication was clear. If Jesus was casting out demons by the Spirit of God, and the kingdom of God had now come upon them, then a dividing line was clearly drawn. We must embrace Jesus *and* His gospel of the kingdom or else we will be working against both. They cannot be divided. To reject Jesus is to reject the kingdom of God as well.

Jesus also cannot be divided from the Spirit of God. To attribute His works to the "Lord of the Flies," was to blaspheme, or speak evil against, the Spirit by whom those works were done. To reject Jesus, as the Pharisees were doing, was to reject the Spirit of God, and there would be no place for them in God's kingdom. With such a stern warning, it was now time for the Pharisees to make a decision. There was nothing halfway about it; it was either all in or all out.

> Either make the tree good and its fruit good, or else make the tree bad and its fruit bad; for a tree is known by its fruit. Brood of vipers! How can you, being evil, speak good things? For out of the abundance of the heart the mouth speaks. A good man out of the good treasure of his heart brings forth

good things, and an evil man out of the evil treasure brings forth evil things. But I say to you that for every idle word men may speak, they will give account of it in the day of judgment. For by your words you will be justified, and by your words you will be condemned. (Matthew 12:33-37)

Up to this point, the Pharisees had shown themselves to be a "brood of vipers" who could not speak anything good about Jesus and the kingdom He preached because their hearts were full of evil. If they did not change their words, they would soon have to give account for them and would be condemned by them. To change their words, they would need to change their hearts and do as Jesus preached from the beginning: "Repent, for the kingdom of heaven is at hand" (Matthew 3:17).

The kingdom of Heaven on Earth is an undivided kingdom. It cannot be separated from Jesus and the Spirit of God. The kingdom of satan is broken. The Lord Jesus has bound him and destroyed his works, and has been loosing his captives ever since.

The Kingdom of the Committed, Not the Curious

While He was still talking to the multitudes, behold, His mother and brothers stood outside, seeking to speak with Him. Then one said to Him, "Look, Your mother and Your brothers are standing outside, seeking to speak with You."

But He answered and said to the one who told Him, "Who is My mother and who are My brothers?" And He stretched out His hand toward His disciples and said, "Here are My mother and My brothers! For whoever does the will of My Father in heaven is My brother and sister and mother." (Matthew 12:46-50)

The scribes and Pharisees witnessed Jesus healing sicknesses and casting out demons. When they objected because He did these things even on the Sabbath, He firmly rebuked them as a "brood of vipers" who spoke evil words because their hearts were evil. But some of them answered,

"Teacher, we want to see a sign from you." They were not talking about the miraculous works He had already performed. They wanted a special sign from heaven just for them, a command performance to confirm to them His authority. Jesus told them,

> *An evil and adulterous generation seeks after a sign, and no sign will be given to it except the sign of the prophet Jonah. For as Jonah was three days and three nights in the belly of the great fish, so will the Son of Man be three days and three nights in the heart of the earth. The men of Nineveh will rise up in the judgment with this generation and condemn it, because they repented at the preaching of Jonah; and indeed a greater than Jonah is here. The queen of the South will rise up in the judgment with this generation and condemn it, for she came from the ends of the earth to hear the wisdom of Solomon; and indeed a greater than Solomon is here. (Matthew 12:39-42)*

Jonah was like Jesus in that he spent three days and nights in the belly of the great fish just as Jesus would be in the heart of the earth for three days and nights. But it was the *message* of Jonah that caused the men of Nineveh to repent. Likewise, it was the *wisdom* of Solomon that caused the Queen of the South to believe God (1 Kings 10:1-9). But someone greater than Jonah and Solomon was now on the scene, and if the scribes and Pharisees were not receptive to His message, they probably would not believe His sign either.

In another place, Jesus said, "My doctrine is not Mine but His who sent Me. If anyone wills to do His will, he shall know concerning the doctrine, whether it is from God or whether I speak on My own authority" (John 7:17). It is not about signs for the curious but about commitment to do God's will. In other words, it is about faith, for without faith it is impossible to please God (Hebrews 11:6). When asked, "What shall we do, that we may work the works of God?" Jesus answered, "This is the work of God, that you believe in Him whom He sent" (John 6:28-29).

If the scribes and Pharisees did not believe in Jesus for who He was and the message He brought, nothing else mattered, no matter how many healings and how many exorcisms He performed. Indeed, the end result would be even worse for them, as Jesus showed them next.

> *When an unclean spirit goes out of a man, he goes through dry places, seeking rest, and finds none. Then he says, "I will return to my house from which I came." And when he comes, he finds it empty, swept, and put in order. Then he goes and takes with him seven other spirits more wicked than himself, and they enter and dwell there; and the last state of that man is worse than the first. So shall it also be with this wicked generation. (Matthew 12:43-45)*

This would be their lot if they refused to believe in Him and let their house be filled with the truth about the kingdom of God.

It was while Jesus was still addressing them that His mother and brothers came, desiring to speak with Him. When informed of this, He said, "Who is My mother, and who are My brothers?" Then He answered His own question. He pointed to His disciples and said, "Here are My mother and My brothers! For whoever does the will of My Father in heaven is My brother and sister and mother."

The condition of the idly curious will go from bad to worse and the judgment upon them will be all the greater because of their persistent unbelief. But the disciples of Jesus, who believe on Him, commit themselves to Him and learn from Him, He will embrace as intimate family.

Whoever does the will of the Father is the brother or sister of Jesus, for His kingdom is all about the will of the Father being done on earth as it is in heaven, and the will of the Father is to believe on the Son.

> *He came to His own, and His own did not receive Him. But as many as received Him, to them He gave the right to become children of God, to those who believe in His name: who were born, not of blood, nor of the will of the flesh, nor of the will of man, but of God. (John 1:11-13)*

He who believes in Him is not condemned; but he who does not believe is condemned already, because he has not believed in the name of the only begotten Son of God. And this is the condemnation, that the light has come into the world, and men loved darkness rather than light, because their deeds were evil. For everyone practicing evil hates the light and does not come to the light, lest his deeds should be exposed. But he who does the truth comes to the light, that his deeds may be clearly seen, that they have been done in God. (John 3:18-21)

The kingdom of Heaven on Earth is not for the curious but for those who have made the commitment of faith in the King.

Parables of Heaven on Earth

And the disciples came and said to Him, "Why do You speak to them in parables?" He answered and said to them, "Because it has been given to you to know the mysteries of the kingdom of heaven, but to them it has not been given. For whoever has, to him more will be given, and he will have abundance; but whoever does not have, even what he has will be taken away from him. Therefore I speak to them in parables, because seeing they do not see, and hearing they do not hear, nor do they understand." (Matthew 13:10-13)

All these things Jesus spoke to the multitude in parables; and without a parable He did not speak to them, that it might be fulfilled which was spoken by the prophet, saying: "I will open My mouth in parables; I will utter things kept secret from the foundation of the world. (Matthew 13:34-35)

Jesus taught in parables. A parable is a figure of speech; it conveys truth about one thing in terms of another. Parables reveal truths about the spiritual realm in terms of the natural realm. The parables of Jesus teach about the kingdom of Heaven on Earth. You might call them "downloads" of the mysteries of the kingdom.

There are those who are ready to receive the kingdom of Heaven on Earth and those who are not. Parables reveal the difference. Those who are ready to receive, believe and obey the words of Jesus will understand the parables, and the mysteries of the kingdom will be revealed to them. For those who are not willing, the kingdom will remain a mystery.

And in them the prophecy of Isaiah is fulfilled, which says:

> *"Hearing you will hear and shall not understand,*
> *And seeing you will see and not perceive;*
> *For the hearts of this people have grown dull.*
> *Their ears are hard of hearing,*
> *And their eyes they have closed,*
> *Lest they should see with their eyes and hear with their ears,*
> *Lest they should understand with their hearts and turn,*
> *So that I should heal them."*
>
> *(Matthew 13:14-15)*

We see a couple of vivid examples of this following the round of parables in Matthew 13. Jesus returned to His hometown, Nazareth, and began teaching in the synagogue. The people were amazed at all He said and did. "Where did this Man get this wisdom and these mighty acts?" (Matthew 13:54). They were confused. They heard the wisdom Jesus spoke and saw that He performed powerful miracles but they did not understand where they came from. They recognized Him only as the carpenter's son; they knew His mother, brothers and sisters—this could not be a prophet of God. So where did He get all these things? Matthew records, "So they were offended at Him" (v. 57). Jesus said, "A prophet is not without honor except in his own country and in his own house" (v. 57) and did not do many miracles there because of their unbelief (v. 58).

In Matthew 14:1-2, we see Herod's reaction to Jesus' ministry. Not long before, he had beheaded John the Baptist. When he heard what Jesus was doing, he said to his servants, "This is John the Baptist; he is risen from the dead, and therefore these powers are at work in him." Herod had rejected the ministry of John and would also soon reject Jesus.

These all saw and heard with their physical senses but they did not *really* see and hear. They had no understanding and they remained in their unbelief. That is why Jesus ends some of His parables with, "He who has ears to hear, let him hear," for whoever has, to him more will be given.

> *But blessed are your eyes for they see, and your ears for they hear; for as-suredly, I say to you that many prophets and righteous men desired to see what you see, and did not see it, and to hear what you hear, and did not hear it. (Matthew 13:16-17)*

The parables of Jesus reveal things that were prophesied in the Old Testament. Saints of old heard and spoke of these things but did not live to see them fulfilled. As the author of Hebrews says, "These all died in faith, not having received the promises, but having seen them afar off were assured of them, embraced them and confessed that they were strangers and pilgrims on the earth" (Hebrews 11:13). But what they saw only afar off is now revealed to us in the parables of Jesus and fulfilled in the kingdom of God—if we have the ears to hear.

THE KINGDOM OF THE SOWER

> *Behold, a sower went out to sow. And as he sowed, some seed fell by the wayside; and the birds came and devoured them. Some fell on stony places, where they did not have much earth; and they immediately sprang up because they had no depth of earth. But when the sun was up they were scorched, and because they had no root they withered away. And some fell among thorns, and the thorns sprang up and choked them. But others fell on good ground and yielded a crop: some a hundredfold, some sixty, some thirty. He who has ears to hear, let him hear! (Matthew 13:3-9)*

Jesus begins this parable with a call to see: "Behold." That is, *See! Here is a figure of earthly things, but look past that to an important spiritual truth.* He ends with a call to hear: "He who has ears to hear, let him hear." Do not just hear the earthly example, listen for the truth in it that comes from heaven. Jesus then explains this parable to His disciples, who were still learning how to see in the spiritual realm and hear the sound of heaven.

Therefore hear the parable of the sower: When anyone hears the word of the kingdom, and does not understand it, then the wicked one comes and snatches away what was sown in his heart. This is he who received seed by the wayside. But he who received the seed on stony places, this is he who hears the word and immediately receives it with joy; yet he has no root in himself, but endures only for a while. For when tribulation or persecution arises because of the word, immediately he stumbles. Now he who received seed among the thorns is he who hears the word, and the cares of this world and the deceitfulness of riches choke the word, and he becomes unfruitful. But he who received seed on the good ground is he who hears the word and understands it, who indeed bears fruit and produces: some a hundredfold, some sixty, some thirty. (Matthew 13:18-23)

The "seed" is the word of the kingdom—the good news that the kingdom of heaven is now here on earth. It is the call to repent and believe, to seek first the kingdom of God and His righteousness. Seed is only part of the equation, however. There must also be good soil in which to sow if there is going to be a harvest of the kingdom. In this parable, there are four kinds of soil, and four kinds of results:

~ First, there are those who hear this good news but do not understand it because they do not receive it in the field of their heart but only along the wayside where the good soil has worn away. Because it cannot take root there, the devil soon comes and snatches it away. We cannot simply tack the kingdom of heaven alongside whatever else we are seeking in life. It must become our priority or else it will be snatched away, and everything else along with it.

~ There are also those who receive the seed and are happy about it, but there are stony places in their heart, just beneath the surface, where they are not willing to yield. Ultimately, the Word cannot be established in them because of their hardness. Their joy and faith soon fades away because they do not let the kingdom dig deep inside them.

~ Then there are those who receive the Word but their heart is full of distracting cares and the temptation to trust in riches. These things have such a stranglehold on them that they are unable to bring forth the good fruit of the kingdom. They do not learn to cast their cares on the Lord who cares for them. They do not make the kingdom of God their priority and therefore do not find all these other things taken care of. They are more like Martha, who was anxious and distracted by many things, instead of like Mary, who chose the "one thing," the "better part" which cannot be taken away (Luke 10:41-42).

~ Finally, there are those who hear the word of the kingdom and give themselves over to it completely. They receive it with the whole heart, letting it deal with all the hard places inside them. The kingdom of God and His righteousness become their priority, the lens through which they view everything else, and everything else is brought into proper perspective. They begin to bring forth the fruit of heaven on earth and it becomes great blessing to others.

Jesus is sowing the word of the kingdom of Heaven on Earth. What kind of soil are you?

THE SONS OF THE KINGDOM

The kingdom of heaven is like a man who sowed good seed in his field; but while men slept, his enemy came and sowed tares among the wheat and went his way. But when the grain had sprouted and produced a crop, then the tares also appeared.

So the servants of the owner came and said to him, "Sir, did you not sow good seed in your field? How then does it have tares?"

He said to them, "An enemy has done this."

The servants said to him, "Do you want us then to go and gather them up?"

But he said, "No, lest while you gather up the tares you also uproot the wheat with them. Let both grow together until the harvest, and at the time of harvest I will say to the reapers, 'First gather together the tares and bind them in bundles to burn them, but gather the wheat into my barn.'" (Matthew 13:24-30)

The previous parable was about four different soils and how they each received the Word of the Kingdom. This parable is about two very different kinds of seed: wheat and tares. Jesus gives us the interpretive key.

He who sows the good seed is the Son of Man. The field is the world, the good seeds are the sons of the kingdom, but the tares are the sons of the wicked one. The enemy who sowed them is the devil, the harvest is the end of the age, and the reapers are the angels. Therefore as the tares are gathered and burned in the fire, so it will be at the end of this age. The Son of Man will send out His angels, and they will gather out of His kingdom all things that offend, and those who practice lawlessness, and will cast them into the furnace of fire. There will be wailing and gnashing of teeth. Then the righteous will shine forth as the sun in the kingdom of their Father. He who has ears to hear, let him hear! (Matthew 13:37-43)

Here is the key:

- ❧ The field = the world.
- ❧ The good seed = the sons of the kingdom.
- ❧ The tares = the sons of the wicked one.

- ❧ The enemy = the devil.
- ❧ The harvest = the end of the age.
- ❧ The reapers = the angels.

Here is how we know that this parable is about the kingdom of heaven *on earth*—there are no tares in heaven. One day there will be no tares at all in the kingdom of Heaven on Earth, but for now, we are living in the in-between time, between Jesus' first coming, when He announced that the kingdom was now here, and His second coming, when it will be here on earth in all its fullness. That is why Jesus taught us to pray, "Kingdom of God, *keep coming*" (the sense of Matthew 6:10).

In the previous parable, satan comes to *snatch away* seed (the Word of the Kingdom). In this parable, satan comes to *sow* seed (tares). The thing about tares is that, when they are young, they look very much like wheat, but when they mature and bear fruit, the difference is quite apparent—and poisonous. What is the difference between the fruit of the tare and that of the wheat? Paul gives us a good example in the contrast between the "works of the flesh" and the "fruit of the Spirit."

Now the works of the flesh are evident, which are: adultery, fornication, uncleanness, lewdness, idolatry, sorcery, hatred, contentions, jealousies, outbursts of wrath, selfish ambitions, dissensions, heresies, envy, murders, drunkenness, revelries, and the like; of which I tell you beforehand, just as I also told you in time past, that those who practice such things will not inherit the kingdom of God.

But the fruit of the Spirit is love, joy, peace, longsuffering, kindness, goodness, faithfulness, gentleness, self-control. Against such there is no law. (Galatians 5:19-23)

James also provides an apt comparison:

Who is wise and understanding among you? Let him show by good conduct that his works are done in the meekness of wisdom. But if you have bitter envy and self-seeking in your hearts, do not boast and lie against the truth. This wisdom does not descend from above, but is earthly, sensual, demonic. For where envy and self-seeking exist, confusion and every evil thing are there.

But the wisdom that is from above is first pure, then peaceable, gentle, willing to yield, full of mercy and good fruits, without partiality and without hypocrisy. Now the fruit of righteousness is sown in peace by those who make peace. (James 3:13-18)

Satan sows his tares to cultivate the works of the flesh and bring forth a wisdom that is full of envy, selfishness, confusion and every evil thing. God is, for the present, allowing it to remain in the field. For the tares get intertwined with the wheat and to remove them too soon would end up damaging the good as well as the bad. That is why, although the kingdom of Heaven on Earth has already begun, we still find evil in the world. But the day is fast approaching when God will send His angels to separate the tares from the wheat, the bad from the good, to destroy that which is evil and preserve that which is good. "Then the righteous will shine forth as the sun in the kingdom of their Father."

A few chapters later, Matthew gives us more insight into this parable. After another exchange with the scribes and Pharisees, this time about the ritual washing of hands (Matthew 15:1-9), Jesus gathered a crowd and began to preach: "Hear and understand: Not what goes into the mouth defiles a man; but what comes out of the mouth, this defiles a man" (vv. 10-11). When His disciples pointed out that this offended the Pharisees, He said, "Every plant which My heavenly Father has not planted will be uprooted. Let them alone. They are blind leaders of the blind. And if the blind leads the blind, both will fall into a ditch" (vv. 13-14). Now the disciples were confused. "Explain this parable to us," they said. Jesus answered,

Do you not yet understand that whatever enters the mouth goes into the stomach and is eliminated? But those things which proceed out of the

mouth come from the heart, and they defile a man. For out of the heart proceed evil thoughts, murders, adulteries, fornications, thefts, false witness, blasphemies. These are the things which defile a man, but to eat with unwashed hands does not defile a man. (Matthew 15:17-20)

The difference between the wheat and tares in the Father's kingdom is a matter of the heart, for the evil that arises in the heart is what defiles a man. Because it does not come from God, it will be uprooted. Let such men alone, Jesus said. Have nothing to do with them. Do not be troubled because they are offended. Their harvest of judgment will come on them soon enough.

The "Word of the Kingdom" produces the sons of the kingdom, bearing the fruit of the Spirit and the wisdom that is from above. Do not worry about the tares; God will deal with them at the appropriate time.

The Kingdom that Starts Small and Finishes Big

Another parable He put forth to them, saying: "The kingdom of heaven is like a mustard seed, which a man took and sowed in his field, which indeed is the least of all the seeds; but when it is grown it is greater than the herbs and becomes a tree, so that the birds of the air come and nest in its branches."

Another parable He spoke to them: "The kingdom of heaven is like leaven, which a woman took and hid in three measures of meal till it was all leavened." (Matthew 13:31-33)

In these two brief parables, Jesus teaches us about the dynamics of the kingdom of Heaven on Earth. In the first one, we see how the mustard seed, though it is very small, becomes a plant large enough to be a tree. In the second, we see how a tiny bit of leaven works through a large batch of dough (the Greek text indicates about half a bushel or more, as much as a woman could knead by herself).

The kingdom of Heaven on Earth starts small and finishes big. That was a surprising twist on Jewish expectations. They knew the kingdom would be large and glorious but they expected that it would burst onto the scene in a great display of political power. What they were *not* expecting was a seed. But in Zechariah, the Lord declared that the things of God do not come about by human power or might but by His Spirit (4:6). Then He said to not despise the day of "small things" (4:10).

The kingdom of Heaven on Earth operates by the power of the Spirit, which is not bound by physical limitations, so size is inconsequential. Even a tiny seed, when it is in the hand of the Lord, becomes a very powerful thing. In Luke 17:21, Jesus tells us that the kingdom is inside of us. How big can that be? Well, consider how much power is packed inside the atom. Though it is microscopically small on the outside, there is an amazing release of energy when it is split. You might say it is bigger on the inside than it is on the outside.

It is the same way with us. We are bigger on the inside than we are on the outside, because the kingdom of God is within and that is enough to change the world. Paul says that God is able to do exceedingly abundantly above all we can ask or think, but he adds that it is according to the power that works in us (Ephesians 3:20). It starts as a small seed within us but soon becomes big enough to change our lives and transform the world.

The kingdom of Heaven on Earth has already begun and has been growing and expanding ever since. As it permeates, its influence is being felt all over the world. It has not yet risen in all its fullness but it is always forcefully advancing, and will continue to do so until King Jesus returns. Then it will shine in all His glory.

THE KINGDOM WORTH EVERYTHING

Again, the kingdom of heaven is like treasure hidden in a field, which a man found and hid; and for joy over it he goes and sells all that he has and buys that field.

Again, the kingdom of heaven is like a merchant seeking beautiful pearls, who, when he had found one pearl of great price, went and sold all that he had and bought it. (Matthew 13:44-46)

The kingdom of Heaven on Earth is like treasure hidden in a field or like a man who finds a pearl beyond compare. One man has not been seeking it at all, but one day he just stumbles across it. Another man has been earnestly seeking after it for years and one glad day happens upon it.

Perhaps the one in the field represents the lowly peasant who had no developed expectation of the messianic kingdom and the merchant stands for one instructed in the Law and the Prophets. Or maybe the merchant signifies the Jews, to whom the promise of the kingdom was made, and the man in the field foreshadows the Gentiles, to whom the Gospel would soon be preached.

Nonetheless, each must make a decision. It is revealed to them suddenly and unexpectedly, in a small moment. But they have "ears to hear" and a heart to receive, so they quickly recognize it for what it is and understand its value. They are overjoyed. Immediately, they give up all they have so they can possess it as their own. Their whole lives have now become all about this wonderful kingdom.

The kingdom of Heaven on Earth is worth everything you have— your whole life.

THE KINGDOM GATHERING IN AND SORTING OUT

Again, the kingdom of heaven is like a dragnet that was cast into the sea and gathered some of every kind, which, when it was full, they drew to shore; and they sat down and gathered the good into vessels, but threw the bad away. So it will be at the end of the age. The angels will come forth, separate the wicked from among the just, and cast them into the furnace of fire. There will be wailing and gnashing of teeth. (Matthew 13:47-50)

Notice that there are two actions taking place in this parable: Gathering in and sorting out. In Matthew 12:32, Jesus spoke of two ages: This age and the age to come. This age is passing away, along with the lust of it (1 John 2:17). It is an age of darkness, but it is fading away and the true light, the light of the age to come, is already shining (1 John 2:8). Those who receive the Lord Jesus are sons of that kingdom which is now breaking into the world. Those who reject Him are part of the world system that is passing away.

This present age is the age of gathering in people of every kind. However, not all who are *in* the kingdom are *of* the kingdom, nor do they all belong *to* the kingdom. There are those to whom the kingdom of Heaven on Earth has been given, and those to whom it has not. There are those who have ears to hear the word of the kingdom and those who do not. There are those who receive the seed in good soil, with the whole heart, and those who do not. There are those who give up everything so that they might possess the kingdom and those who do not. There are those who are "sons of the kingdom," and those who are "sons of the wicked one." In other words, there are those who believe the gospel and receive the King and those who do not.

At the end of this age, there will be a sorting out. Those who belong to the kingdom shall see it in all its fullness and have joy in the age to come. Those who belong to this present age shall see the destruction of all they have so vainly held onto and will know only sorrow and misery.

The kingdom of Heaven on Earth is the only one that is going to be left standing at the end of this age. Be sure that you are not only *in* it, but *of* it, by receiving the King.

The Treasury of the Kingdom

Jesus said to them, "Have you understood all these things?" They said to Him, "Yes, Lord." Then He said to them, "Therefore every scribe instructed concerning the kingdom of heaven is like a householder who brings out of his treasure things new and old." (Matthew 13:51-52)

Having taught His disciples many parables, in public and in private, about the kingdom of Heaven on Earth, Jesus asks them if they understand. The Greek word for "understand" means to put together, to comprehend. "Yes," they answered; they had connected the dots.

Jesus then likened them to scribes. A scribe was a scholar of the Hebrew Scriptures. The disciples already had an understanding about God's purposes in the Old Testament. Maybe not all the *ins* and *outs*, but enough to know about Messiah and His kingdom. Now they were being "instructed"—"discipled" is what the Greek word means—by the King Himself. They were receiving fresh revelation on important aspects of the kingdom they had not known before. They were witnessing the fulfillment of what the ancient prophets had spoken.

Every student of the Old Testament promise who has also been discipled concerning its fulfillment is like the master of the house who "brings out of his treasure things new and old." The treasure, or treasury, is his storehouse; he has laid up for himself treasure in heaven, that which speaks of Heaven on Earth. He "brings out" things "new and old." The Greek word for "bring out" is *ekballo*, which means to fling or hurl forth. It is active, not passive. The master of the house does not wait to be asked but is passionate about taking out this treasure and introducing it to others.

The Greek word for "new" refers to that which is fresh; the word for "old" speaks of that which is ancient, antique, worn by use. For where there is a promise, it must be fulfilled or else it will become stale. "Hope deferred makes the heart sick, but when the desire [that which is hoped for] comes, it is a tree of life" (Proverbs 13:12). The "scribe" discipled in the kingdom of heaven not only brings the hope but also is able to show the fulfillment.

Just as Jesus came preaching the good news of the kingdom of heaven, He prepares His disciples to do the same—to offer the hope of Heaven on Earth and the fulfillment of that hope through faith in Messiah.

The Glory of Heaven on Earth

The kingdom of Heaven on Earth is full of glory. Jesus revealed it by signs, wonders, divine compassion and prophetic insight.

- ❧ The multitudes followed Him out into the wilderness, where, moved with compassion, He healed their sick (Matthew 14:13-14).
- ❧ Then He multiplied fives loaves and two fish to feed them all—five thousand men, besides women and children (Matthew 14:15-21).
- ❧ He walked on the water. Peter did, too, even if only for a moment (14:22-33).
- ❧ He crossed over to Gennesaret, where He healed all who were brought to Him. As many as touched the hem of His garment were made perfectly well (14:34-36).
- ❧ He discerned the hearts of scribes and Pharisees who, by their traditions, set aside the commandments of God. He set aside their particular tradition of washing hands, pointing out that it is not what goes into a man but what comes out of his heart that defiles him (15:1-20).
- ❧ He healed the demon-possessed daughter of a Canaanite woman. Though she was not of Israel, like the Roman centurion

we saw earlier, she possessed great faith (15:21-28).

- He healed the multitudes who came to Him on a mountainside near the Sea of Galilee (Matthew 15:29-31).
- Then He fed them, multiplying seven loaves and a few little fish to satisfy the hunger of four thousand men, besides women and children (15:32-39).
- He discerned the Pharisees and Sadducees, that though they came asking for a sign from heaven, they would not receive one because they stubbornly refused to recognize the sign of the times. He warned His disciples to stay away from the leaven of the Pharisees and Sadducees—the hypocrisy and unbelief that corrupted their teaching (16:1-12).

In Matthew 16-18, the glory of Jesus continues to increase. Peter receives the divine revelation that Jesus is the Messiah, the Son of God. This is the foundation on which Jesus builds His Church, and it overcomes the gates of hell. He releases to the Church the keys of His kingdom—authority to bind on earth what has been bound in heaven and loose on earth what has been loosed in heaven.

The glory of the kingdom is revealed in the Cross of Jesus, and He calls each one of us to take up the cross as we follow Him. Though it seems counter-intuitive, the way to life is found in embracing the symbol of our death, and so the glory of the kingdom is released in us.

The glory of the kingdom is revealed in the Transfiguration, the first of many visions of "the Son of Man coming in His kingdom." It is revealed in all things made possible for those who believe. It is revealed in the revelation that "the sons of the kingdom are free." And it is revealed in the profound dependency and forgiveness to which He calls us.

THE KEYS OF HEAVEN ON EARTH

Jesus answered and said to him, "Blessed are you, Simon Bar-Jonah, for flesh and blood has not revealed this to you, but My Father who is in

heaven. And I also say to you that you are Peter, and on this rock I will
build My church, and the gates of Hades shall not prevail against it. And
I will give you the keys of the kingdom of heaven, and whatever you bind
on earth will be bound in heaven, and whatever you loose on earth will
be loosed in heaven. (Matthew 16:17-19)

Jesus asked His disciples, "Who do men say that I, the Son of Man, am?" After receiving various answers, He then asked, "But who do you say that I am?" Peter boldly answered, "You are the Christ, the Son of the Living God." He nailed it in one, but not because of his own ingenuity—it was a revelation he received from heaven. "Blessed are you, Simon Bar-Jonah, for flesh and blood has not revealed this to you, but My Father who is in heaven."

The kingdom Jesus preached and taught is the connection between heaven and earth. The revelation Peter received on earth came from the Father in heaven. It was the foundational truth that Jesus is the Messiah, the One Anointed by God to redeem His people and be their King. Indeed, Jesus is the Son of the Living God, which is to say that He is the only true God and the source of all life. This powerful truth is the basis for the kingdom of Heaven on Earth.

Jesus said that on this rock, this revelation, He would build His Church, and the gates of hell could not be able to overcome it. The gates of ancient Biblical cities were where the business pertaining to those cities was conducted. They were where counsels were determined and strategies devised. All the plans and devices of hell will never be able to prevail against what Jesus has built on the revelation Peter received about who Jesus is. Indeed, the Church shall overcome and undo all the strategies of hell. For Jesus has given the Church the keys to the kingdom of Heaven on Earth.

Keys control the gates. They open things up and shut things tight. They bind and they loose. The keys of the kingdom are the authority and power to bind on earth what has already been bound in heaven and loose on earth what has already been loosed in heaven. It is not the gates of hell, but the counsels and strategies of heaven, the will of our Father being done on earth as it is in heaven, that will prevail.

THE KINGDOM OF THE CROSS

Then Jesus said to His disciples, "If anyone desires to come after Me, let him deny himself, and take up his cross, and follow Me." (Matthew 16:24)

Peter had just voiced the amazing revelation—directly from the Father—that Jesus is the Messiah, the Son of God. Because of that, Jesus gave him authority to bind and loose on earth what has already been bound and loosed in heaven. But Peter still needed to understand something else, something very important, about this revelation and authority.

After this remarkable exchange, Jesus gave His disciples strict orders *not* to tell anyone that He was the Messiah (Matthew 16:20). Then He began to talk with them about how He must go to Jerusalem, suffer many things from the elders, scribes and chief priest, and then be killed—and raised again the third day (v. 21).

Now they were *really* confused. Wasn't the identity of Jesus as the Messiah to be made known to all? Didn't the coming of Messiah signal that God's triumph was now at hand? Then why such suffering and death, and what did this mean for the kingdom of heaven?

It was more than Peter could take. "Far be it from You, Lord; this shall not happen to You!" he blurted (v. 22). Moments earlier, Peter acknowledged Jesus as the Christ, the Son of God; now he was openly contradicting Him.

Jesus turned to Peter and said, "Get behind Me, Satan! You are an offense to Me, for you are not mindful of the things of God, but the things of men" (v. 23). These were very strong words, but well-deserved. Earlier, Peter had spoken a word directly from heaven, from the mind of God. How quickly he slipped back into the way the world thinks, and suddenly he became the mouthpiece of satan.

God's thoughts are not our thoughts and His ways are not our ways—they are higher (Isaiah 55:8-9). The Jewish expectation was that Messiah would come as a conquering king, a political ruler and military leader; Jesus spoke of a cross and losing one's life.

If anyone desires to come after Me, let him deny himself, and take up his cross, and follow Me. For whoever desires to save his life will lose it, but whoever loses his life for My sake will find it. (Matthew 16:24-25)

A cross is not the reception the world offers a king and his entourage. But Jesus requires that we each embrace the Cross, not just His, but our own. We must disown ourselves in order to follow Him. We must set aside our priorities and interests and seek His. We must give up everything—the whole world—if we would possess His kingdom. We cannot know His life when we are still holding on to our own.

For what profit is it to a man if he gains the whole world, and loses his own soul? Or what will a man give in exchange for his soul? For the Son of Man will come in the glory of His Father with His angels, and then He will reward each according to his works. (Matthew 16:26-27)

The time would shortly come for finding life and rising again, for the glory of God to be revealed and Jesus proclaimed as Messiah. Jesus makes reference here to a prophecy in Daniel:

I was watching in the night visions, and behold, one like the Son of Man, coming with the clouds of heaven! He came to the Ancient of Days, and they brought Him near before Him. Then to Him was given dominion and glory and a kingdom, that all peoples, nations, and languages should serve Him. His dominion is an everlasting dominion, which shall not pass away, and His kingdom the one which shall not be destroyed. (Daniel 7:13-14)

Jesus said, "The Son of Man will come in the glory." A literal rendering of the Greek text is, "is about to be coming." Notice the tenses: "Coming" speaks of a continuous action. "About to be" indicates that it would soon begin.

The kingdom of Heaven on Earth requires a cross for each one of us, that we lose our life for Jesus' sake in order that we may find it. But He also promises great reward, for His kingdom has already begun and will increase until it is here in the fullness of His glory when He returns.

THE SON OF MAN COMING IN HIS KINGDOM

Assuredly, I say to you, there are some standing here who shall not taste death till they see the Son of Man coming in His kingdom. (Matthew 16:28)

Assuredly, I say to you that there are some standing here who will not taste death till they see the kingdom of God present with power. (Mark 9:1)

But I tell you truly, there are some standing here who shall not taste death till they see the kingdom of God. (Luke 9:27)

In all three Gospels, the next event that follows this statement is the Transfiguration. Clearly, the evangelists view that as *a* fulfillment, if not *the* fulfillment, of these words. Peter, James and John were the ones privileged to go with Jesus up on the mount to see Him present in His kingdom and His kingdom present in power.

Now after six days Jesus took Peter, James, and John his brother, led them up on a high mountain by themselves; and He was transfigured before them. His face shone like the sun, and His clothes became as white as the light. And behold, Moses and Elijah appeared to them, talking with Him.

Then Peter answered and said to Jesus, "Lord, it is good for us to be here; if You wish, let us make here three tabernacles: one for You, one for Moses, and one for Elijah."

While he was still speaking, behold, a bright cloud overshadowed them; and suddenly a voice came out of the cloud, saying, "This is My beloved Son, in whom I am well pleased. Hear Him!" (Matthew 17:1-5)

Moses and Elijah appeared with the Lord Jesus there. The revelation of the Old Testament had ended with the admonition to remember the Law of Moses, and the promise that God would send the prophet Elijah before the great "day of the Lord" would arrive. Now Moses and Elijah had come upon the scene—and here was Jesus shining with the glory of heaven!

The disciples were stunned. Mark notes that Peter did not know what to say (Mark 9:6), but that did not keep him from saying it. "Let's make three tabernacles; one for You, one for Moses, and one for Elijah." He completely missed the point. This was not about Moses and Elijah, but about Jesus alone. He was the fulfillment of what the Lawgiver and the Prophet stood for, and when the fulfillment has come, the type is no longer needed. That is why the voice of the Father came from heaven and answered, "This is My beloved Son, in whom I am well pleased. Hear Him!"

At that, the disciples collapsed in awe. Jesus came and touched them, "Arise, and do not be afraid." When they looked up, they saw Jesus only (Matthew 17:6-8). Though they might have great respect for Moses and Elijah, Jesus alone was to be the focus of their attention.

They followed Him back down the mountain and He commanded them, "Tell the vision to no one until the Son of Man is risen from the dead" (v. 9). Mark 9:10 notes, "So they kept this word to themselves, questioning what the rising from the dead meant."

This unusual experience of glory must have raised many questions for them. One they voiced immediately was a question about Elijah. "Why then do the scribes say that Elijah must come first?" (Matthew 17:10). Jesus answered,

Indeed, Elijah is coming first and will restore all things. But I say to you that Elijah has come already, and they did not know him but did to him

whatever they wished. Likewise the Son of Man is also about to suffer at their hands. (vv. 11-12)

"Then the disciples understood that He spoke to them of John the Baptist" (v. 13). Now it clicked for them. John the Baptist was the Elijah whose coming was promised at the end of the Old Testament (Malachi 4:5-6). Luke's Gospel points out this connection when the birth of John the Baptist is foretold to Zacharias: "He will turn many of the children of Israel to the Lord their God. He will also go before Him in the spirit and power of Elijah, 'to turn the hearts of the fathers to the children, and the disobedient to the wisdom of the just to make ready a people prepared for the Lord'" (Luke 1:16-17).

Elijah had come in the person of John, and the way was prepared. But just as John had been rejected, cruelly treated and put to death, so it would also be for Jesus. Again, this was not what the disciples had expected and they still did not fully grasp it, so they did not yet understand what Jesus meant when He said, "until the Son of Man is risen from the dead."

The Transfiguration shows us that this is all about Jesus—His kingdom, His power, His glory. He is the fulfillment of Moses and Elijah—the Law and the Prophets. His disciples saw and experienced this for themselves and it would not be their last time. The other disciples would also see further manifestations of Jesus in His kingdom.

- At the Resurrection, when Jesus was raised by the glory of God and the power of the Holy Spirit.
- At the Ascension, forty days later, when Jesus returned to heaven and took His throne at the right hand of the Father, where He now rules and reigns forever as King over all. Before He ascended, He announced that all authority in heaven and earth had been given to Him, and then commissioned His disciples to proclaim it in all the world.
- At Pentecost, when the Holy Spirit came upon them and they received the very power by which the kingdom operates, to

manifest that Jesus is King. The book of Acts is a chronicle of the kingdom, power and glory of Jesus being put on display. Indeed, the history of the Church is full of such things.

- ☙ At the destruction of Jerusalem and the Temple in AD 70, when Christ revealed Himself in judgment upon the lifeless religious system that had rejected God's Anointed One.

- ☙ At the Second Coming, when the King returns and the *fullness* of His kingdom is made known, and heaven and earth become one. Then *every* eye shall behold Him, *every* knee shall bow and *every* tongue confess that Jesus is Lord.

Do you see Jesus coming in His kingdom—the kingdom of Heaven on Earth? It is the fulfillment of all God promised in the Law and the Prophets, and it has already begun.

The Kingdom Where Nothing is Impossible

Assuredly, I say to you, if you have faith as a mustard seed, you will say to this mountain, "Move from here to there," and it will move; and nothing will be impossible for you. (Matthew 17:20)

Jesus came back down the mountain with Peter, James and John, and a man came up to Him, pleading for his son, a demon-possessed boy who suffered with severe epileptic seizures. He had brought the young man to Jesus' other disciples, but they were unable to heal him (Matthew 17:14-16).

Jesus said, "O faithless and perverse generation, how long shall I be with you? How long shall I bear with you? Bring him here to Me" (v. 17). Jesus located the problem as one of faithlessness, a generation that had turned away. But who was He speaking about?

Perhaps the man himself. In Mark's account, we find him saying to Jesus, "Lord, I believe; help my unbelief!" (Mark 9:24). More likely, though, it was His disciples. After Jesus rebuked the demon and healed the boy, His disciples asked, in private, "Why could we not cast it out?" (Matthew 17:19). Jesus put it on *them*: "Because of your unbelief" (v. 20). The Greek word used for "unbelief" is the same root used for "faithlessness" in verse 17.

The problem was that they were not operating in faith, as they should have been. Eugene Peterson puts it this way in *The Message*, "Because you're not taking God seriously." They still had too much of the world's way of thinking, too much of the world's unbelief at work in them.

Then Jesus showed them the potential of faith, of taking God seriously: "Assuredly, I say to you, if you have faith as a mustard seed, you will say to this mountain, 'Move from here to there,' and it will move; and nothing will be impossible for you" (Matthew 17:20).

Faith is like a seed. It does not have to be big to get a big result, but it does have to be sown, put to work. When you have faith, even a little bit, the exercise of it is simple: You say to the mountain, "Move from here to there," and it will move. However, if there is unbelief going on inside your heart, it will hinder your faith—you have to make a choice to go with one and not the other.

Jesus added, "However, *this kind* does not go out except by prayer and fasting" (v. 21). This kind of *what*? Many people think it refers to the kind of demon that was in the boy. But Jesus did not engage in a lot of praying and fasting when He cast that demon out; He simply rebuked it and it left (v. 18).

The purpose of praying and fasting is not so we can get rid of demons but so we can get rid of unbelief. We know that Jesus had already done a lot of praying and fasting in His life and ministry. He had already dealt with any issues of doubt that tried to creep in on Him (see Matthew 4:1-11, the temptation in the wilderness). Ultimately, unbelief is a tool of the devil, a seed he is always trying to plant in our hearts. Praying and fasting helps us focus on God and hear His Word. Hearing the Word is how faith comes and how it is strengthened in us (Romans 10:17). When we let faith in God fill our hearts, we will leave no place for the doubts of the devil to have a foothold. They get crowded out.

In the kingdom of Heaven on Earth, nothing is impossible when we take God and His promises seriously.

THE SONS OF THE KINGDOM ARE FREE

Then the sons are free. (Matthew 17:26)

When Jesus and His disciples arrived back at Capernaum, men who were in charge of collecting the temple tax came to Peter and asked, "Does your Teacher pay the *double-drachma*?" (Matthew 17:24). Peter answered, "Yes." When he went into the house, Jesus anticipated what he was going to say and stopped him short, "What do you think, Simon? From whom do the kings of the earth take customs or taxes, from their sons or from strangers?" (v. 25).

"From strangers," Peter answered.

Jesus agreed, concluding, "Then the sons are free."

In this little exchange is an amazing teaching about the kingdom of God. The sons of the kings of the earth are exempt from paying taxes, though strangers may still be required to do so. Likewise, the sons of the kingdom of God are not obligated to the Temple. Before the kingdom of God arrived on the scene, the Temple had a specific function as the place of sacrifice and the manifestation of God's presence on earth. Now that the kingdom was at hand in the person of the King, that function was fulfilled and the sons of the kingdom were not bound by it.

Jesus was not against the Temple, but it had served its purpose. Jesus came as the ultimate sacrifice for our sins. The Temple had been a type and a shadow, but now that the fulfillment was here, the shadow no longer served. The author of Hebrews draws the contrast between the earthly Temple and the Tabernacle not made with hands:

We have such a High Priest, who is seated at the right hand of the throne of the Majesty in the heavens, a Minister of the sanctuary and of the true tabernacle which the Lord erected, and not man. (Hebrews 8:10-2)

Christ came as High Priest of the good things to come, with the greater and more perfect tabernacle not made with hands, that is, not of this creation. Not with the blood of goats and calves, but with His own blood He entered the Most Holy Place once for all, having obtained eternal redemption. (Hebrews 9:11-12)

Also implied in Jesus' statement is that those who were obligated to the Temple were not sons of the kingdom but strangers to it. This would refer to the religious leaders and teachers who rejected Jesus—they would have no place in His kingdom. In Matthew 21, after clearing the Temple courts of the moneychangers, Jesus came back into the Temple and confronted the chief priests and elders on the nature of true repentance and their rejection of God's Messiah. He concluded, "Therefore, I say to you, the kingdom of God will be taken from you and given to a nation bearing the fruits of it" (Matthew 21:43). Though they were servants of the Temple, because of their unbelief they were not sons, but strangers to the kingdom of God and to the Temple which foreshadowed it.

In Matthew 24, Jesus predicts the demise of the Temple and the destruction of Jerusalem within a generation (fulfilled in AD 70). In the meantime, although He and Peter were not required to pay the *double-drachma*, they would do so anyway, so that no one would think He despised the Temple itself:

Nevertheless, lest we offend them, go to the sea, cast in a hook, and take the fish that comes up first. And when you have opened its mouth, you will find a piece of money; take that and give it to them for Me and you. (Matthew 17:27)

The Greek for "piece of money" is *stater*, a coin which was equal to two *double-drachmas*, precisely enough to pay the tax for Him and Peter.

In the kingdom of Heaven on Earth, the sons are not bound by types and shadows, or religious systems. We are free to follow the King alone and live fully under His provision.

The Kingdom of Little Ones

At that time the disciples came to Jesus, saying, "Who then is greatest in the kingdom of heaven?"

Then Jesus called a little child to Him, set him in the midst of them, and said, "Assuredly, I say to you, unless you are converted and become as little children, you will by no means enter the kingdom of heaven. Therefore whoever humbles himself as this little child is the greatest in the kingdom of heaven. Whoever receives one little child like this in My name receives Me." (Matthew 18:1-5)

The disciples had been arguing among themselves about who would be the greatest in the kingdom of Heaven on Earth (see Mark 9:33). It was not a discussion about greatness as a matter of character to be emulated but about position to be coveted. They came and asked Jesus.

Jesus turned the question on its head. He set a little child before them. Little children had no status. Their opinions were not solicited and no one sought out their favor. They could not do anything for others; indeed, they were fully dependent on the goodness of others to meet their most basic needs and care for them in every way.

That is how we come into the kingdom of Heaven on Earth, by being fully dependent upon God. It requires a total *re*orientation, a conversion, a turning from faith in us to faith in God. We must become like little children. Without that, we have no place in the kingdom. As Jesus said to Nicodemus, "Unless one is born again, he cannot see the kingdom of God" (John 3:3).

On the other hand, whoever humbles himself to become fully dependent upon God is the greatest in the kingdom. What is more, whoever receives and honors such a one in Jesus' name, receives and honors the Lord Jesus as well. The disciples thought greatness was about pride of position, but it turns out that it is about the humbleness of faith.

This changes everything. No longer are we to live our lives seeking personal power and positions of authority. We come to God confessing,

"I cannot do for myself; You must do for me." It is coming before Him with the meekness and powerlessness of a child. Only these qualify as the ones who are great and worthy of the kingdom. To welcome and honor them in Jesus' name is to welcome and honor Jesus Himself.

So great are these in the eyes of Jesus, He gives stern warnings to those who would treat them in any lesser way: "But whoever causes one of these little ones who believe in Me to sin, it would be better for him if a millstone were hung around his neck, and he were drowned in the depth of the sea" (Matthew 18:6). Offenses will invariably come, but Jesus advises us to do everything necessary to make sure that we are not the offenders (vv. 7-9).

He cautions us, "Take heed that you do not despise one of these little ones, for I say to you that in heaven their angels always see the face of My Father who is in heaven. For the Son of Man has come to save that which was lost" (Matthew 18:10-11). Then He tells the Parable of the Lost Sheep, about the shepherd who has a hundred sheep, but goes out looking for the one that went astray. The lesson is that God is not willing that even one of these "little ones" should perish (vv.12-14). It is a very serious matter to Him.

Everyone who comes depending fully on God belongs to the kingdom of Heaven on Earth, and is to be highly esteemed. Even those whom the world considers the least are among the greatest in God's eyes. Those who despise, hinder or trip them up in any way will face stern judgment from our Father in heaven.

The Kingdom in Jesus' Name

I tell you the truth, whatever you bind on earth will be bound in heaven, and whatever you loose on earth will be loosed in heaven. Again, I tell you that if two of you on earth agree about anything you ask for, it will be done for you by My Father in heaven. For where two or three come together in My name, there am I with them. (Matthew 18:18-20)

Jesus is the connection between heaven and earth. Though He is now seated in heaven at the right hand of the Father, whenever even only two or three come together on earth in His name, He is present. This has everything to do with the kingdom of Heaven on Earth. It is, in fact, the reason given for these two statements:

- ❧ "Whatever you bind on earth will be bound in heaven, and whatever you loose on earth will be loosed in heaven." To bind is to forbid; to loose is to permit. The grammatical tense concerning what is bound or loosed on earth is that they *will already have been bound or loosed* in heaven. That is, whatever we bind on earth *will already have been bound* in heaven, and whatever we set loose on earth *will already have been set loose* in heaven.

- ❧ "If two of you on earth agree about anything you ask for, it will be done for you by My Father in heaven." This second statement is to be taken together with the first statement, about binding and loosing, for it is about manifesting on earth whatever is happening in heaven. Whenever we come into agreement with each other about these things on earth, our Father will bring them about on earth just as they are in heaven.

The particular context of these sayings has to do with resolving disputes among believers (Matthew 18:15-17), but their meaning and application are not limited to that. They are true in particular because they are true in general, for they are in agreement with the general prayer model Jesus gave us to pray, "Your kingdom, come. Your will be done on earth as it is in heaven." Jesus authorizes us to bring forth the will of God on earth just as it is being done in heaven. Not just in certain narrowly defined situations, but in everything that has to do with the heart of our Father in heaven, outside of which there is nothing good.

The authority for these things is the name of Jesus. It is only by coming together in His name that we are able to walk in these things.

To come together in His name means that we are to be all about Him and His purposes, to ask and act on *His* behalf in the way *He* would ask and act. It does no good if we are in agreement with each other but not with Him. It is only as we ask and act in agreement with Him that we able to manifest the will of Heaven on Earth.

THE KINGDOM OF FORGIVENESS ON EARTH

Then Peter came to Him and said, "Lord, how often shall my brother sin against me, and I forgive him? Up to seven times?" Jesus said to him, "I do not say to you, up to seven times, but up to seventy times seven." (Matthew 18:21-22)

Peter figured he would be doing pretty well if he forgave someone seven times. After all, Jewish rule required only three times and Peter was offering seven. He did not realize it, but he was asking a loaded question—and it backfired on him!

"Seven times isn't nearly enough, Peter. Try seventy times seven" (my paraphrase). Jesus wasn't quantifying forgiveness (i.e., forgive 490 times). No, He was saying that there is no limit to forgiveness. Then to drive the point home, He likened the matter of forgiveness to the kingdom of Heaven on Earth—it is vital to our relationship with our heavenly Father.

Therefore the kingdom of heaven is like a certain king who wanted to settle accounts with his servants. And when he had begun to settle accounts, one was brought to him who owed him ten thousand talents. But as he was not able to pay, his master commanded that he be sold, with his wife and children and all that he had, and that payment be made. The servant therefore fell down before him, saying, "Master, have patience with me, and I will pay you all." Then the master of that servant was moved with compassion, released him, and forgave him the debt. (Matthew 18:23-27)

See how great a debt this man was forgiven. Ten thousand talents was an *enormous* amount of money. One talent equaled about 6,000 *denarii*; ten thousand talents was worth 60 million *denarii*. A *denarius* was about one day's wage. If a man labored every day of his life, he would have to work over 164,000 years to pay off such a debt. But that is how much this steward owed his master—and that is how much he was forgiven.

Now, we ought to think that one who was forgiven such a debt would be willing, out of love, respect and gratitude toward his master, to forgive the debt owed him by another. But such was not the case.

> But that servant went out and found one of his fellow servants who owed him a hundred denarii; and he laid hands on him and took him by the throat, saying, "Pay me what you owe!" So his fellow servant fell down at his feet and begged him, saying, "Have patience with me, and I will pay you all." And he would not, but went and threw him into prison till he should pay the debt. (Matthew 18:28-30)

This steward, who was forgiven the debt of 60 million *denarii*, was completely unwilling to forgive the debt of 100 *denarii* (one 600,000th of what he himself had been forgiven). The forgiveness of his master did not penetrate his heart. He did not let even a tiny bit of the kindness shown to him flow through him to someone else.

> So when his fellow servants saw what had been done, they were very grieved, and came and told their master all that had been done. Then his master, after he had called him, said to him, "You wicked servant! I forgave you all that debt because you begged me. Should you not also have had compassion on your fellow servant, just as I had pity on you?" And his master was angry, and delivered him to the torturers until he should pay all that was due to him. (Matthew 18:31-34)

The master had forgiven the great debt owed him, but he expected that the compassion he showed his servant would be reciprocated toward others. Because of his unwillingness to forgive, the servant reaped a hard harvest of suffering and shame.

Now consider carefully Jesus' conclusion to the matter:

So My heavenly Father also will do to you if each of you, from his heart, does not forgive his brother his trespasses. (Matthew 18:35)

Notice that forgiveness is first a matter of the heart. God has forgiven us a great debt, more than we could ever pay, and He intends for it to work throughout our hearts like the leaven of love. When we are unwilling to forgive others, we are rejecting the work God wants to do in us instead of letting divine love have its perfect way. God will not let up on us until we repay the debt of love and forgive those who have sinned against us.

Do not hinder the flow of forgiveness from heaven to earth. Let your love and forgiveness be without limits and so let the heartbeat of your heavenly Father change the world through you. It is vital to the manifestation of Heaven on Earth.

The Incomparable Value of Heaven on Earth

When we make the kingdom of God and His righteousness our priority, He takes care of everything else. Those who give up all for it find life in abundance. This is something the rich young ruler did not understand. He thought he could not afford to sell what he had and give to the poor. He did not realize that he would have experienced the treasure of heaven on earth.

The kingdom of Heaven on Earth is of incomparable value because it is a kingdom of incomparable grace, as the parable of the vineyard shows. As we give ourselves over to the grace of God and begin to learn how to love, give and serve as He does, we discover true greatness in His kingdom.

FOR THE SAKE OF HEAVEN ON EARTH

In Matthew 11, Jesus talked about the kingdom of Heaven on Earth forcefully advancing, and forceful men laying hold of it. In Matthew 13, He described it as a treasure hidden in a field, for which a man would give up all he has in order to possess it as his own. In Matthew 19, He briefly discusses a complication of marriage, particularly concerning divorce. Hearing this, his disciples said, "If such is the case with the man with his wife, it is better not to marry" (v. 10).

But He said to them, "All cannot accept this saying, but only those to whom it has been given: For there are eunuchs who were born thus from their mother's womb, and there are eunuchs who were made eunuchs by men, and there are eunuchs who have made themselves eunuchs for the kingdom of heaven's sake. He who is able to accept it, let him accept it." (vv. 11-12)

Referring to those "who have made themselves eunuchs," He does not mean that they have emasculated themselves, as some have erroneously supposed. Rather, He is speaking of those who choose not to marry but to remain celibate in order to fulfill their destiny in God's kingdom.

Some serve the kingdom by being fruitful and multiplying through marriage and family. Others serve by the devotion and focus unique to those who are single and celibate. Jesus recognized that not all receive this, "but only those to whom it has been given." In other words, it is a special calling. Concerning this same matter, Paul said, "As God has distributed to each one, as the Lord has called each one, so let him walk" (1 Corinthians 7:17), and "Let each one remain in the same calling in which he was called" (v. 20). He cautions that it should not be a matter for great concern, for we are each free to marry or remain single, as the Lord has given us grace.

In the plan of God, the norm is for us to "be fruitful and multiply," to "fill the earth and subdue it," and to "have dominion" (Genesis 1:28). This is the prime directive given to man and woman, and it speaks of uniting in marriage, having children and nurturing families. For those who do, great promise is given:

Behold, children are a heritage from the LORD,
  The fruit of the womb is a reward.
Like arrows in the hand of a warrior,
  So are the children of one's youth.
Happy is the man who has his quiver full of them;
  They shall not be ashamed,
  But shall speak with their enemies in the gate.

(Psalm 127:3-5)

But there is also great promise given to those who follow a special calling, who devote themselves in singleness and celibacy for the sake of the kingdom:

Do not let the son of the foreigner who has joined himself to the LORD *speak, saying, "The* LORD *has utterly separated me from His people;" nor let the eunuch say, "Here I am, a dry tree." For thus says the* LORD*: "To the eunuchs who keep My Sabbaths, and choose what pleases Me, and hold fast My covenant, even to them I will give in My house and within My walls a place and a name better than that of sons and daughters; I will give them an everlasting name that shall not be cut off." (Isaiah 56:3-5)*

So Jesus answered and said, "Assuredly, I say to you, there is no one who has left house or brothers or sisters or father or mother or wife or children or lands, for My sake and the gospel's, who shall not receive a hundredfold now in this time—houses and brothers and sisters and mothers and children and lands, with persecutions—and in the age to come, eternal life. (Mark 10:29-30)

Whether you are married and nurturing children or single and celibate, let it be for the sake of Jesus, the gospel and the kingdom of Heaven on Earth.

THE TREASURE OF HEAVEN ON EARTH

Then Jesus said to His disciples, "Assuredly, I say to you that it is hard for a rich man to enter the kingdom of heaven. And again I say to you, it is easier for a camel to go through the eye of a needle than for a rich man to enter the kingdom of God." (Matthew 19:23-24)

One day a rich young man came to Jesus and asked, "What good thing shall I do that I may have eternal life." He was somehow sensing a lack in his life, a disconnectedness from God, from heaven, even from life itself.

Jesus answered him simply, "If you want to enter into life, keep the commandments." He knew that was where the problem lay and recognized the sort of solution the young man was seeking.

"Which ones?' the young man asked. Jesus named a few, notably, the ones that pertain to relationship with others (the Fifth through Ninth Commandments). "All these things I have kept from my youth," said the young man, and yet he knew that something very important was missing in his life.

Then Jesus gave this startling reply: "If you want to be perfect, go, sell what you have and give to the poor and you will have treasure in heaven; and come, follow Me." The young man went away greatly saddened because he had many possessions. Or as some have noted, his possessions had him.

You see, the real problem was that he was trusting in his possessions, looking to them to be his source and supply. But in so doing, he was breaking the very first commandment: "I am the LORD your God; you shall have no other gods before Me." This young man's wealth and possessions had become his idols, usurping the place of God in his life. He was banking on them, instead of on God, to take care of him.

The young man departed and we do not know whatever became of him. But consider what would have happened if he had believed Jesus and done what He told him. He would have entered into eternal life, the life offered by God, the life Jesus came to bring us in abundance (John 10:10). Not only that, he would have discovered that he could trust God to take care of him and be his source of supply in everything. He would have been banking on heaven.

"You will have treasure in heaven," Jesus said. What is a treasury? It is simply a storehouse. What is the purpose of a storehouse? It is a place where you keep things until you need them. "Treasure in heaven" is not God's way to keep us from the things we need in this life. Quite the opposite, it is how God *preserves* for us the things we need in this life. When we commit ourselves and our means to the kingdom of God and His purposes, thieves cannot break in and steal them, varmints cannot consume them, and rust, rot and mold cannot corrupt them.

Watch how this works: Jesus told the young man to sell what he had and give to the poor, and he would have treasure in heaven. The Bible says, "He who has pity on the poor lends to the LORD, and He will pay back what He has given" (Proverbs 19:17). Perhaps the rich young man forgot this but Jesus did not.

Now, here is an interesting thing about the Hebrew word for "lend," *lavah*. It means to entwine or join together, as in an arrangement between two people. It is used of the relationship between a lender and a borrower. When we give to the poor, God makes a deal with us where we are the lender and He is the borrower. Amazingly, He obligates Himself to us, and He always makes good on His debts. The Hebrew word for "pay back" is *shalam* and, in this arrangement, means that He will reciprocate, recompense, and restore. When God repays, it is always with interest.

If this young man would have sold what he had to sell and given to the poor, he would have had an account with God in the bank of heaven. Then when he himself was in need, God would have repaid him handsomely. But his money and possessions had become his idol, and he trusted in them more than he did in God. And he went away sorrowful.

When we bank our treasure in heaven, God will meet our needs on earth.

THE RECIPROCITY OF HEAVEN ON EARTH

And everyone who has left houses or brothers or sisters or father or mother or wife or children or lands, for My name's sake, shall receive a hundredfold, and inherit eternal life. (Matthew 19:29)

After the rich, young man departed, Jesus discussed the matter with His disciples: "Assuredly, I say to you that it is hard for a rich man to enter the kingdom of heaven. And again I say to you, it is easier for a camel to go through the eye of a needle than for a rich man to enter the kingdom of God" (Matthew 19:23-34).

The disciples were greatly amazed. "Who then can be saved?" They had assumed that material prosperity meant God's blessing was on a person. After all, Psalm 112:3 says that wealth and riches will be in the house of those who love and serve the Lord. That is true enough, but it is not a guarantee that those who are rich are also faithful.

The promise is for those who love, trust and serve God. Those who love trust, and serve money may experience wealth and riches for a season but it will not last because it is out of order—it is not true prosperity. Those who love and trust in their riches, as this young man did, do not enter the kingdom of heaven. The disciples were astonished by Jesus' statement because they still had too much of the world's way of thinking in them. It was a puzzlement: "Who then can be saved?"

Jesus looked directly at them and answered, "With men this is impossible, but with God all things are possible" (v. 26). Impossible, yet possible—a paradox. It is impossible for those who trust in their riches, yet possible for those who trust in God. The young man's problem was not that he was rich but that he loved his possessions more than he desired God. He cared more about his wealth than he did about eternal life.

Remembering what Jesus instructed the young man, "Sell what you have and give to the poor," Peter saw hope, a way for the impossible to become possible: Let go of riches and embrace the way of God. "See, we have left all and followed You," he said, "Therefore, what shall we have?" If the rich young man had done as Jesus said, and followed Him, he would have entered into the kingdom of heaven. Even though Peter and the disciples did not have the same wealth the young man possessed, they did give up everything to follow Jesus. Surely, that would mean *something*, wouldn't it? He was beginning to see that it is not what you have but who you trust that makes all the difference. Jesus answered:

Assuredly I say to you, that in the regeneration, when the Son of Man sits on the throne of His glory, you who have followed Me will also sit on twelve thrones, judging the twelve tribes of Israel. And everyone who has left houses or brothers or sisters or father or mother or wife or children or lands, for My name's sake, shall receive a hundredfold, and inherit eternal life. (Matthew 19:28-29)

"Assuredly" indicates that this is a key truth, vital to our basic understanding concerning the kingdom of Heaven on Earth. The "regeneration" Jesus is talking about is not the individual "born again" experience he spoke of to Nicodemus. No, He was talking about the "new birth" of the world, the spiritual transformation that would begin when Jesus, the Son of Man, ascended to the "throne of His glory." Not only would He be sitting on His throne, the place of ruling and reigning over His kingdom, but those who follow Him would also be seated on thrones to rule and reign with Him.

When would this take place? When the Son of Man is enthroned in glory. When will *that* happen? It has happened already! It happened forty days after the Resurrection, at what is called the Ascension. The Son of Man ascended to heaven and was seated on His throne at the right hand of the Father, "far above all principality and power and might and dominion, and every name that is named, not only in this age but also in that which is to come" (Ephesians 1:21). Paul tells us that we have been seated there as well (Ephesians 2:6).

Though the rule and reign of Jesus and all His disciples has not yet been fully manifested in the earth, it has already begun. We see it, for instance, in the authority Jesus gives us in Matthew 18:18: "Assuredly, I say to you, whatever you bind on earth will be bound in heaven, and whatever you loose on earth will be loosed in heaven." And in John 20:23: "If you forgive the sins of any, they are forgiven them; if you retain the sins of any, they are retained." And in the Great Commission, where Jesus declared:

> *All authority has been given to Me in heaven and on earth. Go therefore and make disciples of all the nations, baptizing them in the name of the Father and of the Son and of the Holy Spirit, teaching them to observe all things that I have commanded you; and lo, I am with you always, even to the end of the age. (Matthew 28:18-20)*

By binding and loosing, and bringing the Gospel of Forgiveness to

Israel and the nations, the disciples of Jesus exercise the rule and authority of Heaven on Earth.

Now notice what else Jesus said in answer to Peter's question: "Everyone who has left houses or brothers or sisters or father or mother or wife or children or lands, for My name's sake, shall receive a hundredfold, and inherit eternal life." This, likewise, is not just about the age to come, but about *this* life, for the age to come is now breaking into this present age. The parallel account in Mark's Gospel makes this clearer:

Assuredly, I say to you, there is no one who has left house or brothers or sisters or father or mother or wife or children or lands, for My sake and the gospel's, who shall not receive a hundredfold now in this time— houses and brothers and sisters and mothers and children and lands, with persecutions—and in the age to come, eternal life. (Mark 10:29-30)

The rich young man came to Jesus seeking eternal life. Jesus told him to sell what he had, give to the poor and follow Him—to leave it all behind for the sake of Jesus and the gospel. But his eyes were too fixed on this age and all its ways to see that God's kingdom was breaking into the world. He would have had a hundredfold return of whatever he left behind—*now in this time*—as well as eternal life in the age to come.

It is the reciprocity of Heaven on Earth. When we make the kingdom of God and His righteousness our priority, everything else will be added to us. Whatever we let go for the sake of His kingdom, we will receive again a hundred times over.

The Grace of Heaven on Earth

The kingdom of heaven is like a landowner who went out early in the morning to hire laborers for his vineyard. (Matthew 20:1)

After the encounter with the rich young man, and Jesus' discussion with His disciples about it afterwards, Jesus segued into another parable of the kingdom. The narrative begins and ends with this paradox: "But many who are first will be last, and the last first" (Matthew 19:20) and "So the last will be first, and the first last" (Matthew 20:16). The parable in between (Matthew 20:1-15) shows how this surprising turn-around takes place.

In this parable the landowner went out at about 6 a.m., hired a group of laborers for a *denarius* a day (the standard wage), and put them to work. At 9 a.m., he went and hired another group, saying, "Whatever is right I will give you." Though they had no reason to expect a full day's pay, since they would not be giving a full day's work, they had every right to expect the standard wage pro-rated to them. At noon, the landowner went out again and did the same. Then at 5 p.m., an hour before quitting time, he hired one last little group, saying, "What is right, you will receive."

Finally, evening came, and it was time for all the workers to be paid. The landowner had them line up to receive their wages. He paid the last ones first. To their surprise and delight, the latecomers each received a *denarius*—a full day's pay. Now, the ones who had worked the full day, seeing this, supposed that since the last ones were receiving the full wage, the first ones would be receiving that and more. But to their surprise and chagrin, they each received a *denarius*—and nothing more.

How they complained about the landowner! They felt cheated and abused. "These last men have worked only one hour, and you made them equal to us who have borne the burden and the heat of the day."

Hearing one of them grumble, the landowner answered him directly. "Friend, I am doing you no wrong. Did you not agree with me for a denarius? Take what is yours and go your way. I wish to give to this last man the same as to you. Is it not lawful for me to do what I wish with my own things? Or is your eye evil because I am good?"

The truth is that he had wronged nobody; he simply showed goodness to those who needed it. Because of his generosity, those who earlier were content to receive a full day's wage for a full day's work now felt they deserved more. They became greedy and jealous.

Jesus concluded the parable with this: "So the last will be first, and the first last." There are those who think they should be valued more because they are first and others who believe they are worth less because they are last. But they are all the same with God. He cares just as much about the poor and helpless as He does the rich and powerful. In the kingdom of God, it is never a question about our worthiness but about His grace. Even those hirelings who labored the whole day were the recipient's of grace, for the landowner was under no obligation to hire them in the first place. It was his favor that had given them a paying job.

The rich young man, whose encounter led to this parable, thought he was ready to pursue eternal life, but the thing that gave him prominence in the world turned out to be the very thing that held him back because he was unwilling to let it go. On the other hand, Jesus' desire was for him to remember the poor, who have nothing but God to lean on. "Blessed are the poor in spirit, for theirs is the kingdom of heaven." The "poor in spirit" are those who realize they have nothing except God, but they also know that He is more than enough—something the rich young man failed to understand. So the last indeed become first, and the first last.

Those who hold onto position, possessions and the pride of being first may end up with nothing. Those who let go of these things and trust in the goodness and grace of God will always have enough and more.

THE KINGDOM OF SERVANT GREATNESS

Whoever desires to become great among you, let him be your servant ...
just as the Son of Man did not come to be served, but to serve, and to give
His life a ransom for many. (Matthew 20:26, 28)

On the heels of the parable of the landowner and the laborers, Matthew records this account, where the symbolic language of parable gets fleshed out in the example of Christ:

Now Jesus, going up to Jerusalem, took the twelve disciples aside on the road and said to them, "Behold, we are going up to Jerusalem, and the Son of Man will be betrayed to the chief priests and to the scribes; and they will condemn Him to death, and deliver Him to the Gentiles to mock and to scourge and to crucify. And the third day He will rise again." (Matthew 20:17-19)

Here is Jesus, preeminent as king in His own kingdom, giving Himself over to be treated as anything but king. He is rightfully the first and the greatest but He trades that for the place of the least and the lowest. The first was willing to become last that the last might become first. But that is not the end of the reversal. Because He joined Himself with the last, God performed the greatest reversal of all, making Jesus the first above all firsts.

Let this mind be in you which was also in Christ Jesus, who, being in the form of God, did not consider it robbery to be equal with God, but made Himself of no reputation, taking the form of a bondservant, and coming in the likeness of men. And being found in appearance as a man, He humbled Himself and became obedient to the point of death, even the death of the cross. Therefore God also has highly exalted Him and given Him the name which is above every name, that at the name of Jesus every knee should bow, of those in heaven, and of those on earth, and of those under the earth, and that every tongue should confess that Jesus Christ is Lord, to the glory of God the Father. (Philippians 2:5-11)

There is more to reflect on in this story, however, for the mother of James and John came to see Jesus:

Then the mother of Zebedee's sons came to Him with her sons, kneeling down and asking something from Him. And He said to her, "What do you wish?"

She said to Him, "Grant that these two sons of mine may sit, one on

Your right hand and the other on the left, in Your kingdom." (Matthew 20:20-21)

The request actually came from James and John, as the parallel account in Mark 10:35-45 shows, but they enlisted the help of their mother. They were seeking the place of preeminence, the place of being first—greatness in the kingdom of Heaven on Earth. The lesson of the parable had not yet penetrated their hearts for, clearly, they did not yet comprehend the true nature of what they were asking.

But Jesus answered and said, "You do not know what you ask. Are you able to drink the cup that I am about to drink, and be baptized with the baptism that I am baptized with?"

They said to Him, "We are able."

So He said to them, "You will indeed drink My cup, and be baptized with the baptism that I am baptized with; but to sit on My right hand and on My left is not Mine to give, but it is for those for whom it is prepared by My Father." (Matthew 20:22-23)

James and John answered accurately, though not out of understanding, and Jesus recognized it as prophetic: Not only were they able, but they would indeed do so. But what they wanted was not in Jesus' hand to give, but the Father's. For Jesus did not even seek to exalt Himself, but was exalted by the Father.

Now, the other disciples caught wind of what James and John had done, and the situation might have turned ugly—as if the others did not desire the same thing for themselves—except that Jesus took it as an opportunity to enlighten them on the nature of true greatness, making explicit what had been veiled in the previous parable.

And when the ten heard it, they were greatly displeased with the two brothers. But Jesus called them to Himself and said, "You know that the rulers of the Gentiles lord it over them, and those who are great exercise authority over them. Yet it shall not be so among you; but whoever desires to become great among you, let him be your servant. And whoever desires to be first among you, let him be your slave—just as the Son of Man did not come to be served, but to serve, and to give His life a ransom for many." (Matthew 20:24-28)

Jesus turned everything upside down. In the world of the Gentiles, greatness was about being able to lord oneself and exercise authority over others, and the disciples had been infected with that kind of thinking. But it is not so in the kingdom of Heaven on Earth, where those who desire to be first must be willing to become last and those who want to be great must take on the role of the servant.

Carefully note what Jesus is saying but also what He is not saying. He is not saying how to become great, He is describing greatness itself! That is, He is not telling us how, by serving others, we can eventually rise to the place of greatness where we no longer need to serve but can exercise authority over others. That's a power trip that comes from the bowels of hell, not the heart of the Father. No, Jesus is teaching us that serving others is itself greatness. Paradoxically, when we take the place of the servant and become the last, we become the first, for the first is the servant of all.

It is the way of God Himself. I call it the *algebra of love*: God is love; love gives and serves. God so loved the world that He gave His only Son (John 3:16). It is the way of Jesus, for He did not come to be served— to lord it over people and exercise authority over them—but to serve. Not only to serve, but to give up His life for the sake of others. It is as an obedient bondservant that He has been highly exalted by God and given the name that is above every name.

Jesus, who made Himself the last, the servant of all, has been made "the firstborn from the dead, that in all things He may have the preeminence" (Colossians 1:18). God has raised Him from the dead and seated Him at the right hand of the Father, "far above all principality and power and might and dominion, and every name that is named, not only in this age, but also in that which is to come" (Ephesians 1:20-21). Not only that, Paul teaches us that God has also made us (believers in Jesus) alive together with Christ, and raised us up together "and made us sit together in the heavenlies in Christ Jesus" (Ephesians 2:5-6).

Notice the time and place. The verbs are in the past tense. That is, they do not describe a future event for which we wait, but an accomplished fact, a present reality out of which we live. We are *now* seated with Christ in the heavenlies. Where is He seated? At the right hand of the Father, far above all principality, power, might and dominion. Then that is exactly where the Father has seated us, too—at His right hand, far above all principality, power, might and dominion. Isn't that what James and John desired?

Greatness in the kingdom of Heaven on Earth is about being a servant. For we rule and reign with Jesus, the Servant King, and "as He is, so are we in this world" (1 John 4:17).

The Controversial Kingdom

As the glory of Jesus and His kingdom was revealed more and more, it became increasingly controversial. This opposition arose mostly from the Jewish leaders—the scribes, Pharisees, chief priests and Sadducees. Jesus is a threat to the traditions and power structures of the religious spirit. In the end, He denounced these religious leaders for their great hypocrisy. Jesus is looking for faith, the fruit of repentance and honest love for God and man, which fulfills all the Law and the Prophets.

THE KING ANOINTED FOR ALL

Hosanna to the Son of David!
"Blessed is He who comes in the name of the LORD!"

(Matthew 21:9)

Jesus came into Jerusalem riding on a donkey. Though this may seem odd to us today, it carried great significance back then. Matthew, in his characteristic way of linking prophecy with fulfillment, quotes Zechariah 9:9, a text concerning the Messiah:

All this was done that it might be fulfilled which was spoken by the prophet, saying:

"Tell the daughter of Zion,
'Behold, your King is coming to you,
Lowly, and sitting on a donkey,
A colt, the foal of a donkey.'"

(Matthew 21:4-5)

In this instance, entering Jerusalem on the back of a humble donkey identified Jesus, not just as *a* king, but as *the* King, the Son of David who would fulfill the royal lineage. He was entering as Messiah—the Anointed One.

None of this was lost on the multitudes, which went before and after Him crying out, "Hosanna to the Son of David! Blessed is He who comes in the name of the Lord!" They were quoting Psalm 118, a key passage for the annual Passover pilgrimage. "Hosanna" is from the Hebrew and means "Save now."

Save now, I pray, O LORD;
O LORD, send now prosperity.
Blessed is He who comes in the name of the LORD!

(Psalm 118:25-26)

The crowds recognized Jesus as the long-promised King of Israel, the Anointed One who was to deliver them and restore to them the blessings of covenant relationship with God. They were exuberant in their celebration.

Matthew continues this theme as he takes us into the next scene, the Temple, where Jesus overturns the tables of the moneychangers and the seats of those who sold doves, saying, "It is written, 'My house shall be called a house of prayer,' but you have made it a den of thieves" (v. 13).

Jewish law required that a half-shekel be given in tribute by every man over twenty years old. The moneychangers served to convert the various currencies into what was required for this temple tax. The dove-sellers provided animals for the poor to be able to bring a sacrifice to the house of God, as provided for in the law. These were not inappropriate activities of themselves, and deserving of reasonable fees, although some, no doubt, would take advantage of the pilgrims.

Jesus charged them with making the house of prayer into a "den of thieves," but overcharging travelers was not their greatest robbery. The verse He quotes is very significant here "For My house shall be called a house of prayer *for all nations*" (Isaiah 56:7). Matthew leaves out "for all nations," but Mark includes it in his parallel account (Mark 11:17). The "nations" refers to the Gentiles, the "foreigners" who were outside of the divine covenant, but whom God greatly desired to bring in:

> *Also the sons of the foreigner*
> > *Who join themselves to the LORD, to serve Him,*
> *And to love the name of the LORD, to be His servants—*
> > *Everyone who keeps from defiling the Sabbath,*
> *And holds fast My covenant—*
> > *Even them I will bring to My holy mountain,*
> *And make them joyful in My house of prayer.*
> > *Their burnt offerings and their sacrifices*
> *Will be accepted on My altar;*
> > *For My house shall be called a house of prayer for all nations.*
> > > *(Isaiah 56:6-7)*

The problem with the moneychangers was not so much *what* they were doing as *where* they were doing it. They set up shop in the outer courts of the Temple, in the section reserved for the Gentiles. This "Court of the Gentiles" was established so that they, too, could come and honor the God of Israel. But the money handlers and dove merchants conducted business with little regard that the sprawling commotion hindered what little opportunity the Gentiles were given to worship. The Father's house was to be a house of prayer for *all* nations and these merchants were robbing them, turning it into a den of thieves by their activity. With righteous indignation, Jesus called them on it. Mark tells us that the scribes and chief priests wanted to destroy Him for that (Mark 11:18).

Jesus was not quite through offending the Temple authorities, though. Next came the blind and the lame to be healed by Him—right there in the Temple. Old Testament law prohibited blind and lame priests from serving in the Temple, but religious tradition expanded this ban to exclude all the blind and lame in general from entering in. But Jesus received them gladly into His Father's house and healed them. The scribes and chief priests could not complain about this openly, but inwardly they seethed.

That is not all that had them angry. There were also children who came into the Temple and cried out the same thing that the multitudes had cried out in the streets: "Hosanna to the Son of David" (Matthew 21:15). The scribes and priests were incensed. They went to Jesus and said, "Do you hear what these are saying?" They knew full well what the significance was—and coming from the mouths of children, who were not even supposed to be in the Temple. But Jesus made room for the children just as He did for the Gentiles, and the blind and lame. He answered the scribes and priests and brought them up short:

Yes. Have you never read,

> *"Out of the mouth of babes and nursing infants*
> *You have perfected praise"?*
>
> *(Matthew 21:16)*

He was quoting Psalm 8:2, which is about praise given only to God. But the children were speaking it about Jesus, and Jesus received it, in effect acknowledging He is God.

When Jesus came into Jerusalem that final week, He presented Himself as King, Messiah and God. He was anointed, not just for some, but for all—from the humblest child to the greatest nation. None is excluded; all who come to Him by faith may enter into His kingdom.

The Kingdom of Repentance and Fruit

Therefore I say to you, the kingdom of God will be taken from you and given to a nation bearing the fruits of it. (Matthew 21:43)

J esus is looking for fruit in His kingdom, in the spiritual as well as in the natural. The narrative of the fig tree gives us a natural example that is loaded with spiritual significance.

Now in the morning, as He returned to the city, He was hungry. And seeing a fig tree by the road, He came to it and found nothing on it but leaves, and said to it, "Let no fruit grow on you ever again."

Immediately the fig tree withered away. And when the disciples saw it, they marveled, saying, "How did the fig tree wither away so soon?"

So Jesus answered and said to them, "Assuredly, I say to you, if you have faith and do not doubt, you will not only do what was done to the fig tree, but also if you say to this mountain, 'Be removed and be cast into the sea,' it will be done. And whatever things you ask in prayer, believing, you will receive. (Matthew 21:18-22)

Jesus was hungry, so He went to the fig tree looking for a little fruit to eat. The fact that there were leaves on the tree indicated that there should also have been figs, even if nothing more than small, unripe but edible ones. Though the leaves offered the promise of fruit, when Jesus came to the tree, He discovered there was actually none at all. So He spoke to the tree and said, "Let no fruit grow on you ever again," and it immediately began to wither.

The disciples were amazed and Jesus used this as an opportunity to teach them an important kingdom principle about the operation of faith: When we have faith and do not doubt, whatever we say will be done. A corollary to this is that whatever things we ask in prayer, if we ask in faith, we will receive it. (See also Mark 11:22-24).

That is certainly a powerful lesson but it does not exhaust the significance of this story, for Jesus was looking for fruit in the spiritual realm, as the rest of Matthew 21 demonstrates. The next thing Matthew records is that Jesus went to the Temple, where the chief priests and elders came up and asked, "By what authority are You doing these things? And who gave You this authority?" (Matthew 21:23). Jesus turned the question around on them:

> I also will ask you one thing, which if you tell Me, I likewise will tell you by what authority I do these things: The baptism of John—where was it from? From heaven or from men?" (vv. 24-25).

John the Baptist had come preaching a baptism of repentance with a call to "bear fruits worthy of repentance" (Matthew 3:8), but the chief priests and elders rejected him. Now they were in a bind. If they said that John's baptism was authorized by heaven, they knew Jesus' follow-up would be, "Then why didn't you believe him?" On the other hand, they were afraid to stand before the crowd and say that John's baptism was merely a human contrivance because the people recognized John as a prophet of God. They were in a *double* bind. So they said, "We do not know." Though they had expected an honest answer from Jesus, they we not willing to tell the truth about themselves.

Just as Jesus had turned their question around on them, now He turned their answer around on them: "Neither will I tell you by what authority I do these things" (Matthew 21:27). They had presented themselves as being concerned about matters of authority, but it turns out that this was merely a front for a different agenda. If they had truly cared about divine authority, they would have listened to John and brought forth the fruits of repentance. Though they tried to hide behind their dishonesty, they were exposed for what they truly were.

But Jesus was not yet finished with them. He set them up again with this parable:

> But what do you think? A man had two sons, and he came to the first and

said, 'Son, go, work today in my vineyard.' He answered and said, 'I will not,' but afterward he regretted it and went. Then he came to the second and said likewise. And he answered and said, 'I go, sir,' but he did not go. Which of the two did the will of his father? (Matthew 21:28-31)

The chief priest and elders walked right into it and answered, "The first." Then Jesus drove it home on them.

Assuredly, I say to you that tax collectors and harlots enter the kingdom of God before you. For John came to you in the way of righteousness and you did not believe him; but tax collectors and harlots believed him; and when you saw it, you did not afterward relent and believe him. (Matthew 21:31-32)

There are those who put on a good religious front but are so caught up in their own sense of righteousness that they long ago ceased to hear and obey the Lord. They speak the right words, and commend themselves for it, but they do not follow through. They are like the fig tree that put forth leaves, promising fruit, but then turned out to be barren.

On the other hand, there are those who may be considered the vilest of sinners, who flout the commands of God, but then bring forth the fruits of repentance and faith. They are like the first son. By recognizing that it was the repentant son who actually ended up doing the will of God, the chief priests and elders condemned themselves. They knew what the truth was but were so disconnected from it, they did not realize that they were the disobedient ones.

But Jesus is still not finished, He has another parable for them. This one is about a landowner who established a vineyard, complete with hedging, a winepress and a watchtower. Then he leased it to vinedressers and went away to a far country. At harvest time, he sent his servants to receive his fruit, but the vinedressers beat one of them, stoned another and killed a third. The patient landowner sent another group of servants, who received the same treatment. Finally, the landowner sent his son, saying, "The will respect my son," but the vinedressers cast him out of the vineyard and killed him.

At this point in the story, Jesus stopped and asked, "Therefore, when the owner of the vineyard comes, what will he do to those vinedressers?" (Matthew 21:40). The chief priests and elders, oblivious to their role in this parable, quickly gave their answer: "He will destroy those wicked men miserably, and lease his vineyard to other vinedressers who will render to him the fruits in their seasons" (v. 41).

They walked right into it once again, condemning themselves by their own words. Jesus turned it around on them a third time:

Have you never read in the Scriptures:

> *"The stone which the builders rejected*
> *Has become the chief cornerstone.*
> *This was the LORD's doing,*
> *And it is marvelous in our eyes"?*

Therefore I say to you, the kingdom of God will be taken from you and given to a nation bearing the fruits of it. And whoever falls on this stone will be broken; but on whomever it falls, it will grind him to powder. (Matthew 21:42-43)

Jesus is looking for fruit. Not for fig trees that promise fruit by their leaves but then fail to produce. Not for sons who offer lip service but then do not obey. Not for vinedressers who strike a deal but then refuse to yield what rightfully belongs to the landowner. Nor for priests and Pharisees who put on a pious show but then fail to believe those whom God has sent. The kingdom of God is taken away from them and they will be destroyed by that which they have rejected.

No, Jesus is looking for those who come humbly before Him and bring forth fruits worthy of repentance, the ones who, regardless of their former disobedience, turn and obey the truth. The kingdom of God belongs to them, for they turn out to be the ones Jesus spoke of from the beginning: "Blessed are the poor in spirit, for theirs is the kingdom of heaven" (Matthew 5:3).

The kingdom of Heaven on Earth belongs to those who bring forth the fruits of repentance, faith and obedience.

THE KINGDOM OF THE CHOSEN

For many are called but few are chosen. (Matthew 22:14)

Many get invited; only a few make it. (The Message)

By now, the chief priests and Pharisees had begun to catch on that Jesus was speaking about them. He gives them this final parable about entering into the kingdom of Heaven on Earth:

The kingdom of heaven is like a certain king who arranged a marriage for his son, and sent out his servants to call those who were invited to the wedding; and they were not willing to come. Again, he sent out other servants, saying, "Tell those who are invited, 'See, I have prepared my dinner; my oxen and fatted cattle are killed, and all things are ready. Come to the wedding.'" But they made light of it and went their ways, one to his own farm, another to his business. And the rest seized his servants, treated them spitefully, and killed them.

But when the king heard about it, he was furious. And he sent out his armies, destroyed those murderers, and burned up their city. Then he said to his servants, "The wedding is ready, but those who were invited were not worthy. Therefore go into the highways, and as many as you find, invite to the wedding." So those servants went out into the highways and gathered together all whom they found, both bad and good. And the wedding hall was filled with guests.

But when the king came in to see the guests, he saw a man there who did not have on a wedding garment. So he said to him, "Friend, how did you come in here without a wedding garment?" And he was speechless. Then the king said to the servants, "Bind him hand and foot, take him away, and cast him into outer darkness; there will be weeping and gnashing of teeth." For many are called, but few are chosen. (Matthew 22:2-14)

At the conclusion of the parable, Jesus asks them no questions, rhetorical or otherwise. The meaning is plain enough. They know well enough that He is talking about them, though they would, no doubt, take great exception to it. But they are like the wicked vinedressers of the previous parable, who killed the servants and son of the landowner. And now, in this parable, they are like those who were invited but who disregarded the royal invitation, and some even killed the king's servants. Jesus later speaks to the scribes and Pharisees, no longer in parables, which offered them an opportunity to repent, but indicts them directly:

Woe to you, scribes and Pharisees, hypocrites! Because you build the tombs of the prophets and adorn the monuments of the righteous, and say, "If we had lived in the days of our fathers, we would not have been partakers with them in the blood of the prophets." Therefore you are witnesses against yourselves that you are sons of those who murdered the prophets. Fill up, then, the measure of your fathers' guilt.

Serpents, brood of vipers! How can you escape the condemnation of hell? Therefore, indeed, I send you prophets, wise men, and scribes: some of them you will kill and crucify, and some of them you will scourge in your synagogues and persecute from city to city, that on you may come all the righteous blood shed on the earth, from the blood of righteous Abel to the blood of Zechariah, son of Berechiah, whom you murdered between the temple and the altar. (Matthew 23:29-35)

God gave an invitation to come celebrate His Son, an invitation to the "wedding feast" (foreshadowing the "marriage supper of the Lamb" in Revelation 19:9). But the religious leaders mostly ignored and rejected it, sometimes violently, even killing His prophets. They were not very happy about the Son, either, and wanted to kill Him as well.

In the parable, the king was not pleased; he had the murderers destroyed and their city burned. Then, since those he had originally invited would not come, he had his servants go out where the crowds were and gather people in to fill up the wedding hall. A great honor, which was initially shown only to a few, was now extended to all.

This corresponds with history, for the Jewish leaders did indeed reject Jesus, the Son of God, and had Him crucified. Within a generation, their city, Jerusalem, was burned in AD 70. Meanwhile, the invitation of the Gospel was offered to all, Jew and Gentile alike.

In the parable, the guests show up, but the king notices one who has not dressed appropriately. It was often the custom when kings and community leaders hosted such wedding events to supply their guests with robes befitting the occasion. But here was a man who, though he did not reject the invitation to come, decided that his own garments would be good enough. He was summarily ejected.

There are many people who are called to God's feast, but who want to come on their own terms. God has provided robes of righteousness for them but they believe their own righteousness is sufficient. It is not. Commenting on the most outwardly righteous of men in Israel, Jesus said, "For I say to you, that unless your righteousness exceeds the righteousness of the scribes and Pharisees, you will by no means enter the kingdom of heaven" (Matthew 5:20).

Our own righteousness is not enough and never could be. But God has provided us with the appropriate garment to attend His feast—His own righteousness:

For He [God] made Him who knew no sin [Christ] to be sin for us, that we might become the righteousness of God in Him. (2 Corinthians 5:21)

The invitation has been extended. The garments have been supplied. All that is left is for us to come and receive.

The kingdom of Heaven on Earth is a kingdom of the chosen. The invitation is given to all but we each must respond by faith, receiving the righteousness of Christ. Many are called, but only those who believe are chosen.

The Kingdom of Divine Authority

Render therefore to Caesar the things that are Caesar's, and to God the things that are God's. (Matthew 22:21)

Stinging from the truth of the parables Jesus told about them, the Pharisees seethed and plotted how they might "entangle Him in His talk" (Matthew 22:15). So they sent their disciples, along with the political/religious group known as the Herodians, to set Jesus up for a takedown.

First, they tried to oil Him with smooth words: "Teacher, we know that You are true, and teach the way of God in truth; nor do You care about anyone, for You do not regard the person of men. Tell us, therefore, what do You think? Is it lawful to pay taxes to Caesar, or not?" (v. 16-17).

This was a very controversial matter. The Herodians wanted authority over Jerusalem to be fully restored to the Herods, as it once had been, instead of being governed by Pontius Pilate. They were not much interested in paying Roman taxes. Then there were the Zealots, who absolutely despised Rome and certainly wanted no part of paying her taxes.

But Jesus knew what they were up to. "Why do you test Me, you hypocrites? Show Me the tax money."

They brought Him a foreign coin with Caesar's image. Coins minted in Judea, though they were Roman, bore no such image. Paying Roman taxes with a coin bearing Caesar's inscription would have been all the more offensive.

"Whose image and inscription is this?" He asked.

"Caesar's," they said.

"Render therefore to Caesar the things that are Caesar's, and to God the things that are God's." This was not merely a clever answer to avoid a direct response. It drove home an important point they had hoped to avoid: there are indeed governing authorities to whom we owe certain obligations.

The Jews had long recognized that God is the one who establishes kingdoms and authorities as well as brings them down. The history of Israel, particularly Babylonian captivity and exile, had proven that God would raise up authorities over her when she strayed from His ways. Now they were living under Roman rule and forced to pay Caesar's tax, and they divided over whether it was right, according to their law, to do so.

The Pharisees and Herodians had already answered it for themselves; it was no mere coincidence that they had the coin with Caesar's inscription at hand. God had raised up an authority over the Jews, but were they willing to confess that they had once again strayed from the Lord? That was the challenge Jesus' answer now posed. They were stunned. His answer was a wonder to them, forcing them to either surrender to Him or else deny what they knew to be the truth. The only response they gave was to walk away (v. 22).

Jesus' statement raises questions for us as well. How does the kingdom of heaven relate to governing authorities on earth? Exactly what obligations do we, as subjects of His kingdom, owe them?

First, we must understand that God and Caesar are not equal authorities in our lives. Not by a long shot. God is sovereign over all, but in His sovereignty, He has chosen to set up rulers and governments. That Caesar has any authority at all is dependent upon God. That we render anything to Caesar at all is because we first render everything to God. Any obligation we might owe Caesar is merely a small part of the obedience we owe God. Where there is a conflict between the commandments of God and the laws of men, we must always obey God. For the authority of God is absolute, the authority of men is subservient to divine sovereignty.

In addition to the words of Jesus, here is more of what the Bible has to say about how we are to relate to government:

Let every soul be subject to the governing authorities. For there is no au-thority except from God, and the authorities that exist are appointed by God. Therefore whoever resists the authority resists the ordinance of God, and those who resist will bring judgment on themselves. For rulers are not a terror to good works, but to evil. Do you want to be unafraid of the authority? Do what is good, and you will have praise from the same. For he is God's minister to you for good. But if you do evil, be afraid; for he does not bear the sword in vain; for he is God's minister, an avenger to execute wrath on him who practices evil. Therefore you must be subject, not only because of wrath but also for conscience' sake. For because of this you also pay taxes, for they are God's ministers attending continually to this very thing. Render therefore to all their due: taxes to whom taxes are due, customs to whom customs, fear to whom fear, honor to whom honor. (Romans 13:1-7)

Therefore I exhort first of all that supplications, prayers, intercessions, and giving of thanks be made for all men, for kings and all who are in authority, that we may lead a quiet and peaceable life in all godliness and reverence. (1 Timothy 2:1-2)

Therefore submit yourselves to every ordinance of man for the Lord's sake, whether to the king as supreme, or to governors, as to those who are sent by him for the punishment of evildoers and for the praise of those who do good. (1 Peter 2:13-14)

What then is our obligation?

- ❧ *Pay your taxes.* We do receive benefits from God-ordained gov-ernment and it is only right that we should pay our fair share. Better yet, *give* your taxes. Don't send them in grudgingly; bless it to the government. Pray over it and task it with the purpose of heaven. Let it proclaim that our God is mighty. Let it prophesy the kingdom of Heaven on Earth. This requires faith.

ֆ *Obey the government in every good thing.* God ordained it, not to terrorize good, but to protect from evil. Therefore, keep doing good in all things. We cannot submit to doing evil but we can always do what is good and right.

ֆ *Pray and intercede for the government and its leaders.* Praise God for them and for the purpose for which He ordained them. If they are not obeying that purpose, pray for God to bring them to repentance and spiritual awakening. Ask and believe God to raise up righteous leaders who hear His voice and walk in His ways, in all three branches and at all levels of government.

We must yield, first and always, to the authority of God. But we must also yield to the subservient authorities He has established among men, except where they are in conflict with His ways. For the kingdom of God is all about His will being done on earth as it is in heaven.

THE KINGDOM OF THE LIVING

God is not the God of the dead, but of the living. (Matthew 22:32)

The scribes and Pharisees were very angry with Jesus, but the Sadducees also had a bone to pick with Him. Two of their distinctives were that they did not believe in the resurrection of the dead, and the only Hebrew Scriptures they accepted as divine were the first five books of Moses. After the Pharisees had a go at Jesus, the Sadducees came to test Him with this scenario:

Teacher, Moses said that if a man dies, having no children, his brother shall marry his wife and raise up offspring for his brother. Now there were with us seven brothers. The first died after he had married, and having no offspring, left his wife to his brother. Likewise the second also, and the third, even to the seventh. Last of all the woman died also. Therefore, in the resurrection, whose wife of the seven will she be? For they all had her. (Matthew 22:24-28)

Jesus unraveled their assumptions, pointing out all the ways their understanding was deficient:

You are mistaken, not knowing the Scriptures nor the power of God. For in the resurrection they neither marry nor are given in marriage, but are like angels of God in heaven. But concerning the resurrection of the dead, have you not read what was spoken to you by God, saying, "I am the God of Abraham, the God of Isaac, and the God of Jacob"? God is not the God of the dead, but of the living. (Matthew 22:29-32)

- First, they did not comprehend the truth of the Scriptures, not even the ones they claimed to accept, the books of Moses.
- Second, they did not realize the power of God. They had become so worldly-minded they came to believe that this short life is all we get, that God would not or could not reconstitute bodies which had long returned to dust. But surely that would be no problem for the God who spoke all creation into existence at the beginning, as Moses taught.
- Third, they also did not understand that life in the resurrection will not be like the present. Marriage, which the Sadducees thought presented a huge problem according to their scenario, will not even be an issue. In the resurrection, the mandate to be fruitful and multiply (Genesis 1:28) will have already been fulfilled.
- Finally, they totally missed the significance of the words God spoke to Moses: "I am the God of Abraham, the God of Isaac, and the God of Jacob" (Exodus 3:6, 16). He did not say "I *was* the God of Abraham," but "I *am*," and therein lies the argument. It means that, as Jesus concluded, God is not the God of the dead, but of the living. Therefore, those who have

gone from this earth still live, but there will be a bodily resurrection, for God created us to dwell in bodies on earth.

When Lazarus died, Jesus came and assured Martha that he would rise again. She said, "I know that he will rise again in the resurrection at the last day." This was the common faith of the Jews, except for the Sadducees, and was intimated throughout the Hebrew Scriptures. Jesus said to her, "I *am* the resurrection and the life. He who believes in Me, though he may die, he shall live. And whoever lives and believes in Me shall never die. Do you believe this?" (John 11:25-26).

God is the God of the living and His kingdom is eternal. At the end of the book of Revelation, we see heaven and earth joined together forever, the eternal dwelling place for all the resurrected saints.

Now I saw a new heaven and a new earth, for the first heaven and the first earth had passed away. Also there was no more sea. Then I, John, saw the holy city, New Jerusalem, coming down out of heaven from God, prepared as a bride adorned for her husband. And I heard a loud voice from heaven saying, "Behold, the tabernacle of God is with men, and He will dwell with them, and they shall be His people. God Himself will be with them and be their God. And God will wipe away every tear from their eyes; there shall be no more death, nor sorrow, nor crying. There shall be no more pain, for the former things have passed away." (Revelation 21:1-4)

The kingdom of Heaven on Earth is eternal. Those who belong to it, through faith in Jesus Christ, who is the resurrection and the life, have passed from death unto life. Do you believe this?

THE KINGDOM WHERE LOVE FULFILLS ALL

When the Pharisees heard that He had silenced the Sadducees, they gathered together. Then one of them, a lawyer, asked Him a question, testing Him, and saying, "Teacher which is the greatest commandment in the law?"

"You shall love the Lord your God with all your heart, with all your soul, and with all your mind." This is the first and great commandment. And the second is like it: "You shall love your neighbor as yourself." On these two commandments hang all the Law and the Prophets. (Matthew 22:37-40)

The Pharisees and Sadducees had both made a run at trapping Jesus in His words—and failed. Now came an expert in the Law of Moses, not to ensnare him, as the others had done, but to examine his teaching. Mark's Gospel refers to him as a scribe: "Then one of the scribes came, and having heard them reasoning together, perceiving that He had answered them well, asked Him, "Which is the first commandment of all?" (Mark 12:28). It was common for Jews to discuss which were the weightier matters of the law.

"You shall love the Lord your God with all your heart, with all your soul, and with all your mind," Jesus answered. "This is the first and great commandment." This was first, not in order of time, but of importance.

"And the second is like it: 'You shall love your neighbor as yourself.'" If the most important commandment is about loving God, then the second must be about loving man, who was created in the image and likeness of God. The second commandment is not separate from the first, but extends from the first. One cannot keep the first without also keeping the second. John said that whoever loves God must also love his brother (1 John 4:20).

Then Jesus concluded with the importance of these two commandments: "On these two commandments hang all the Law and the Prophets." That is, everything in the Law and the Prophets—all of the Old Testament—is about these two things.

Remember that the Ten Commandments were given on two tables of stone (Exodus 31:18). Many commentators believe that the first tablet spoke of our obligation toward God, the second of our obligation toward others. When we love God we will have no other gods before us, we will not try to fashion Him according to our own ideas, we will not speak His name in vanity, idleness or arrogance, and we will honor that which He has set apart unto Himself. When we love our neighbor as ourselves, we will give proper honor to those who have fathered and mothered us; we will not take the lives of our neighbors into our own hands; we will not violate their marriage covenants; we will not take from them what is rightfully theirs; we will not lie against them; and we will not crave for ourselves that which belongs exclusively to them. All the Law is about loving God and loving all others as ourselves. As Paul notes, following in the footsteps of Jesus, "Love is the fulfillment of the law" (Romans 13:10).

It is not just the Law that hangs on these two great commandments but the Prophets also. Both the Law and the Prophets are all about the kingdom of heaven—the rule and reign of God in the affairs of men. These are the two commandments of the kingdom of Heaven on Earth. Everything else depends on and is understood by them.

Think back to the rich young man who came to Jesus seeking eternal life. Jesus asked if he knew the commandments, then named some of them, particularly the ones from the second tablet, the ones about loving one's neighbor as oneself. "I have kept all of these from my youth," the young man answered. We already know that he really had not learned to keep the first tablet, to love the Lord his God with all his heart, soul and mind; he loved his possessions too much for that. As it turns out, he also did not keep the second tablet either, though he was sure he had. He did not love his neighbor as himself or else he would have listened to Jesus when He told him to sell what he had and give to the poor. Not understanding that the intent of the Law was about love, he missed out on everything.

The lawyer who asked which was the greatest commandment was strongly impressed by Jesus' answer. "Well said, Teacher. You have spoken the truth, for there is one God, and there is no other than He. And to love Him with all the heart, with all the understanding, with all the soul, and with all the strength, and to love one's neighbor as oneself, is more than all the whole burnt offerings and sacrifices" (Mark 12:32-33).

Jesus answered, "You are not far from the kingdom of God" (Mark 12:34). The truth of His answer was backed up by the strength of His love.

In the kingdom of Heaven on Earth, the commandment to love fulfills everything else.

THE KINGDOM OF THE SON OF GOD

While the Pharisees were gathered together, Jesus asked them, saying, "What do you think about the Christ? Whose Son is He?"

They said to Him, "The Son of David."

He said to them, "How then does David in the Spirit call Him 'Lord,' saying: 'The LORD said to my Lord, "Sit at My right hand, till I make Your enemies Your footstool"'? If David then calls Him 'Lord,' how is He his Son?'

And no one was able to answer Him a word, nor from that day on did anyone dare question Him anymore. (Matthew 22:41-46)

The Pharisees and Sadducees had asked Jesus a number of questions. Now He had a question for *them* concerning the Messiah: "Whose Son is He?"

They had a ready answer: "The Son of David." It was the standard answer, safe and acceptable, and quite correct as far as it went. But now Jesus asked the tough question with which they had not really wrestled: "How then does David in the Spirit call Him 'Lord'?"

Jesus quoted Psalm 110, a messianic psalm written by David under the inspiration of the Holy Spirit. There David stated, "The LORD said to my Lord …" (v. 1). That is, David referred to Messiah as "my Lord," recognizing Him as his master. But how could Messiah be both David's son and David's master? That was one aspect of the puzzle.

Another aspect was that David recognized this as an accomplished fact, not a future event. Notice the tense. He did not say, "The LORD *will say* to my Lord," but "The LORD *said* to my Lord." That is, David not only recognized that Messiah was his superior, but also that He somehow already existed. How could that be, unless Messiah was divine, a being from eternity? A few verses later, David said, "The LORD has sworn and will not relent, 'You are a priest *forever* according to the order of Melchizedek'" (Psalm 110:4).

The Jews were aware of this conundrum but had not been able to work it out. But now here was Jesus standing before them as both the Son of David and the Son of God. That blew their circuits. They had no answer, and they did not ask any more questions, perhaps because they were not willing to follow wherever the answers might lead.

The kingdom of Heaven on Earth is the kingdom of Messiah, Son of David and Son of God.

HINDRANCES TO THE KINGDOM

Woe to you, scribes and Pharisees, hypocrites! For you shut up the kingdom of heaven against men; for you neither go in yourselves, nor do you allow those who are entering to go in. (Matthew 23:13)

The scribes and Pharisees had given up on trying to entangle Jesus in their controversies and discredit Him in the eyes of the people. Jesus, however, was not yet finished with them and He now gave His assessment of them before the people. He had long been aware of what they were about, what motivated them and how they operated. He even hinted at it when He preached The Sermon of Heaven on Earth. What He had veiled then, He now made explicit in His public denunciation of them.

He recognized that they sat in "Moses' seat," that is, they had spiritual authority in the synagogue system. "Therefore whatever they tell you to observe, that observe and do," He said, and then added, "But do not do according to their works; for they say, and do not do" (Matthew 23:3). Then he began to enumerate:

For they bind heavy burdens, hard to bear, and lay them on men's shoulders; but they themselves will not move them with one of their fingers. But all their works they do to be seen by men. They make their phylacteries broad and enlarge the borders of their garments. They love the best places at feasts, the best seats in the synagogues, greetings in the marketplaces, and to be called by men, "Rabbi, Rabbi." (Matthew 23:4-7)

The scribes and Pharisees loved to do their works to be seen and praised of men. They put on a good show, making a theatre of their "devotion" to wow the crowds. They were all about themselves, not the kingdom of heaven. Jesus had no kind words for them, but labeled them for what they were: play-acting, mask-wearing hypocrites. Then He pronounced a series of "woes" on them (Matthew 23:13-32):

- Woe to you, scribes and Pharisees, hypocrites! For you shut up the kingdom of heaven against men; for you neither go in yourselves, nor do you allow those who are entering to go in.

- Woe to you, scribes and Pharisees, hypocrites! For you devour widows' houses, and for a pretense make long prayers. Therefore you will receive greater condemnation.

- Woe to you, scribes and Pharisees, hypocrites! For you travel land and sea to win one proselyte, and when he is won, you make him twice as much a son of hell as yourselves.

- Woe to you, blind guides, who say, "Whoever swears by the temple, it is nothing; but whoever swears by the gold of the temple, he is obliged to perform it." Fools and blind! For which is greater, the gold or the temple that sanctifies the gold? And, "Whoever swears by the altar, it is nothing; but whoever swears by the gift that is on it, he is obliged to perform it." Fools and blind! For which is greater, the gift or the altar that sanctifies the gift? Therefore he who swears by the altar, swears by it and by all things on it. He who swears by the temple, swears by it and by Him who dwells in it. And he who swears by heaven, swears by the throne of God and by Him who sits on it.

ॐ Woe to you, scribes and Pharisees, hypocrites! For you pay tithe of mint and anise and cummin, and have neglected the weightier matters of the law: justice and mercy and faith. These you ought to have done, without leaving the others undone. Blind guides, who strain out a gnat and swallow a camel!

ॐ Woe to you, scribes and Pharisees, hypocrites! For you cleanse the outside of the cup and dish, but inside they are full of extortion and self-indulgence. Blind Pharisee, first cleanse the inside of the cup and dish, that the outside of them may be clean also.

ॐ Woe to you, scribes and Pharisees, hypocrites! For you are like whitewashed tombs which indeed appear beautiful outwardly, but inside are full of dead men's bones and all uncleanness. Even so you also outwardly appear righteous to men, but inside you are full of hypocrisy and lawlessness.

ॐ Woe to you, scribes and Pharisees, hypocrites! Because you build the tombs of the prophets and adorn the monuments of the righteous, and say, "If we had lived in the days of our fathers, we would not have been partakers with them in the blood of the prophets." Therefore you are witnesses against yourselves that you are sons of those who murdered the prophets. Fill up, then, the measure of your fathers' guilt.

Jesus was not condemning all scribes and Pharisees. As we saw earlier, there was at least one to whom Jesus said, "You are not far from the kingdom of God." There were probably others like that as well. What Jesus was denouncing, however, was the attitude that prevailed among them, a self-righteousness and self-aggrandizement that corrupted everything they did. This attitude not only kept them from receiving the kingdom of Heaven on Earth, it also hindered others from entering it. Apart from the kingdom, all that was left for them was judgment.

Serpents, brood of vipers! How can you escape the condemnation of hell? Therefore, indeed, I send you prophets, wise men, and scribes: some of them you will kill and crucify, and some of them you will scourge in your synagogues and persecute from city to city, that on you may come all the righteous blood shed on the earth, from the blood of righteous Abel to the blood of Zechariah, son of Berechiah, whom you murdered between the temple and the altar. Assuredly, I say to you, all these things will come upon this generation

O Jerusalem, Jerusalem, the one who kills the prophets and stones those who are sent to her! How often I wanted to gather your children together, as a hen gathers her chicks under her wings, but you were not willing! See! Your house is left to you desolate. (Matthew 23:33-39)

This did indeed come to pass within a generation, when Jerusalem and the Temple were destroyed in AD 70.

Do not let self-righteousness and hypocrisy, neither yours nor that of anybody else, keep you from entering the kingdom of Heaven on Earth.

Heaven on Earth and the End of the Age

In Matthew 24-25, Jesus teaches the disciples about Heaven on Earth and the end of the age. He answers their questions: "When will these things be? And what will be the sign of Your coming, and of the end of the age?" (Matthew 24:3). Then He instructs them on how to be prepared for that time.

THE GOSPEL OF THE KINGDOM

And this gospel of the kingdom will be preached in all the world as a witness to all the nations, and then the end will come. (Matthew 24:14)

In Matthew 23, Jesus denounced the scribes and Pharisees because of their great hypocrisy. He pronounced a series of woes upon them, ending with the judgment that would soon befall Jerusalem because of her corrupt leadership. In Matthew 24:1-2, Jesus speaks also of the coming destruction of the Temple. For the Jewish mind, the Temple would stand as long as the world endured—its destruction would signal the end of the age. Recognizing the import of Jesus' warning, the disciples asked, "When will these things be? And what will be the sign of Your coming, and of the end of the age?" (v. 3).

The balance of chapter 24 is Jesus' answer. As with many prophecies in the Bible, there may be something of a double fulfillment in view, one sooner, one later, with an indiscernible length of time in between. Exactly where the overlap occurs, where one fulfillment ends and the other begins has been the subject of much controversy among Bible interpreters.*

Most are generally agreed that the Roman destruction of Jerusalem in AD 70 is at least a partial or initial fulfillment. God poured out His judgment on the Temple system and the faithless Jewish leadership that rejected Messiah and the sacrifice He made. This destruction made the Temple sacrifices no longer possible but also underscored the truth that the Cross had already rendered them unnecessary.

Leading up to this destruction, Jesus warned that many would come, claiming to be Messiah, and would deceive many (v. 4-5). Josephus Flavius, Jewish historian of the first century, reports that there were many messianic pretenders during this period. Eusebius, early Church historian, also documents this.

Jesus said the disciples would hear of wars and the threat of wars, that nation would rise up against nation, and that there would be famines, pestilences and earthquakes in various places (vv. 6-8). All these things happened, as the annals of Rome amply record. The book of Acts speaks of a great famine and Josephus details a terrible famine that occurred during this period. Pompeii was shaken by earthquake in AD 62. These are just a few examples.

---

* My viewpoint on Matthew 24 is non-dispensational. That is, it is not the understanding that has been popularized by the recent *Left Behind* series. It is generally in line with the theological viewpoints known as *historic premillennialism, amillennialism* and *postmillennialism*. It is also known as *partial preterism* (note the *partial*). If this chapter gets your interest in learning more about these positions, here are a few books for further study. Harold R. Eberle and Martin Trench, *Victorious Eschatology: A Partial Preterist View*, Second edition (Yakima, WA: Worldcast, 2006). This covers Matthew 24 extensively. Eberle is a historic premillennialist; Trench is postmillennial. Keith A. Mathison, *Postmillennialism: An Eschatology of Hope* (Phillipsburg, NJ: P&R Publishing, 1999). This is a general presentation of postmillennialism and partial preterism, with a brief analysis of Matthew 24. Kim Riddlebarger, *A Case for Amillennialism: Understanding the End Times* (Grand Rapids: Baker Books, 2003). Chapter 13 deals with the Olivet Discourse (the teaching of Jesus in Matthew 24, Mark 13 and Luke 21) and offers an exposition on Matthew 24. R. C. Sproul, *The Last Days According to Jesus: When Did Jesus Say He Would Return?* (Grand Rapids: Baker Books, 1998). Mostly a consideration of the Olivet Discourse from a postmillennial, partial preterist viewpoint.

All these would be just the beginning of sorrows, Jesus said. His disciples would be delivered up, persecuted and killed for His sake (v. 9). We see this fulfilled in the book of Acts and in early Church history. Many were offended at their witness, and hated them. The early Church was persecuted by both the Jews and the Romans.

False prophets would come and deceive many. Lawlessness would increase and the love of many would grow cold (v. 10-12). Paul and John, in their letters, addressed the beginning stages of Gnosticism, a doctrine which often led to lawlessness. In the book of Revelation, John admonished the church at Ephesus for leaving her "first love," and the author of Hebrews exhorted his readers, who were experiencing increasing persecution, not to pull away from their faith in Christ.

Jesus promised that "he who endures to the end shall be saved" (v. 13). Though many were turning away, those who remained in the faith would be delivered. They would see the fulfillment: "This gospel of the kingdom will be preached in all the world as a witness to all the nations, and then the end will come" (v. 14) The "end" He speaks of is the "end of the age," for that is what the disciples were asking. But which age was He talking about? The age of the old covenant, including the Law of Moses, the Temple and the sacrifices. It was about to end; its purpose had been fulfilled.

God created Israel and covenanted with her to be a "kingdom of priests" (Exodus 19:6) whose purpose was to represent Him before the nations and the nations before Him, bringing forth the Word of God and revealing Messiah to the world. Though the accompanying religious system had become corrupted by unbelief, encrusted with human tradition, and the ruling Jewish authorities failed to recognize the Messiah, God's purpose would be fulfilled nonetheless and the gospel of His kingdom would be "preached in all the world as a witness to the nations." The Greek word for "world" here is *oikoumene*, which often referred to the known world, for example, the Roman Empire (Luke 2:1; Acts 11:28; Acts 17:6; Acts 24:5). Paul, especially called by God to be an evangelist to the Gentiles (the nations), demonstrates the reach of the gospel throughout the Empire:

I thank my God through Jesus Christ for you all, that your faith is spoken of throughout the whole world. (Romans 1:8)

But I say, have they not heard? Yes indeed: "Their sound has gone out to all the earth, and their words to the ends of the world." (Romans 10:18)

Now to Him who is able to establish you according to my gospel and the preaching of Jesus Christ, according to the revelation of the mystery kept secret since the world began but now made manifest, and by the prophetic Scriptures made now to all the nations. (Romans 16:25-26)

Because of the hope which is laid up for you in heaven, of which you heard before in the word of the truth of the gospel, which has come to you, as it has also in all the world, and is bringing forth fruit. (Colossians 1:5-6)

The hope of the gospel which you heard, which was preached to every creature under heaven. (Colossians 1:23)

Paul was martyred about AD 67. Within a few years of the gospel spreading out across the Roman Empire, Jerusalem and the Temple were destroyed and the age of the old covenant system was complete.

There is yet another fulfillment of this prophecy, though, for there is yet another age that must pass away. It is the present world system of which satan is the god (2 Corinthians 4:4). It has its own wisdom that is opposed to the wisdom of God, but God shows it to be foolishness (1 Corinthians 3:19). The Lord Jesus Christ "gave Himself for our sins, that He might deliver us from this present evil age" (Galatians 1:4). This age is being overtaken by the age of God's kingdom, which has been forcefully advancing ever since Jesus came. As the apostle John said, "The darkness is passing away and the true light is already shining" (1 John 2:8).

The gospel of the kingdom will continue to be preached as a witness to all the nations, for Paul said, "Blindness in part has happened to Israel until the fullness of the Gentiles [nations] has come in. And so all Israel will be saved" (Romans 11:25-26). The nations shall be redeemed and Israel shall embrace her Messiah. Thus comes the end of this present evil age, for the kingdom of Heaven on Earth will then be here in all its fullness.

The King Coming in Judgment

There are many aspects to the coming judgment on Jerusalem and the Temple. Jesus warns of the "abomination of desolation," of "great tribulation" and false messiahs. He foretells the *sign* of the Son of Man and His coming, and then gives the time-stamp for when these things would occur.

Abomination of Desolation

Therefore when you see the "abomination of desolation," spoken of by Daniel the prophet, standing in the holy place (whoever reads, let him understand), then let those who are in Judea flee to the mountains. Let him who is on the housetop not go down to take anything out of his house. And let him who is in the field not go back to get his clothes. But woe to those who are pregnant and to those who are nursing babies in those days! (Matthew 24:15-19)

The "abomination of desolation" refers to an abomination that would cause desolation or destruction. The Greek word for "abomination" speaks of loathing or repugnance. There was something coming that would be very repugnant to the people and would bring destruction. The "holy place" refers to the city of Jerusalem, as we see in Luke's parallel account:

But when you see Jerusalem surrounded by armies, then know that its desolation is near. Then let those who are in Judea flee to the mountain, let those who are in the midst of her depart, and let not those who are in the country enter her ... And they will fall by the sword, and be led away captive into all nations. And Jerusalem will be trampled by Gentiles until the times of the Gentiles are fulfilled. (Luke 21:20-21)

We also see here that the abomination that causes desolation would be the armies the surrounded the city. In Spring of AD 67, Nero commissioned Vespasian to go up against Jerusalem. Thus began a siege which culminated three and a half years later when the city was finally destroyed in August of AD 70. Thousands upon thousands of Jews were crucified, many others were killed or died of starvation, and those who were left were carried off into slavery. Jerusalem was trampled underfoot by the Roman legions and left desolate. However, even while the Roman armies were surrounding the city, there was still time for those who believed Jesus' warning to escape to the countryside.

Great Tribulation

And pray that your flight may not be in winter or on the Sabbath. For then there will be great tribulation, such as has not been since the beginning of the world until this time, no, nor ever shall be. And unless those days were shortened, no flesh would be saved; but for the elect's sake those days will be shortened. (Matthew 24:20-22)

Jesus warned them of a coming tribulation that would be very severe, unlike any that had ever been experienced before, or would be after. He was still speaking about the desolation of Jerusalem. The Jews were massacred on a scale they had never before known. Josephus describes it in horrendous detail. They suffered atrocities, not only at the hands of the Romans, but also by other Jews. Famine was so severe because of the siege, cannibalism erupted throughout the city to the extent that mothers were killing and eating their own children. Though the Holocaust of Hitler's Germany was greater in magnitude, in terms of covenantal significance, there was no comparison. For the Jews, the destruction of the Temple was the end of the world. After earlier destructions in 583 BC and 163 BC, they had been able to rebuild, but since it was obliterated in AD 70, *the Temple has never been built again.*

False Messiahs to Come

Jesus promised that the days of great tribulation would be shortened for the sake of the elect, but He also warned them that false messiahs would appear.

> *Then if anyone says to you, "Look, here is the Christ!" or "There!" do not believe it. For false christs and false prophets will rise and show great signs and wonders to deceive, if possible, even the elect. See, I have told you beforehand. Therefore if they say to you, "Look, He is in the desert!" do not go out; or "Look, He is in the inner rooms!" do not believe it. For as the lightning comes from the east and flashes to the west, so also shall the coming of the Son of Man be. For wherever the carcass is, there the eagles will be gathered together. (Matthew 24:23-26)*

Josephus records that many false messiahs did arise in those days, even working signs and wonders. But the coming that Jesus was talking about would not happen in secluded places or hidden rooms—the disciples should not look for Him there. It would be very evident to all. However, as we shall see in the Parable of the Fig Tree, this is not the Second Coming that is spoken of elsewhere in the New Testament. Rather, it is the judgment of Christ coming like lightning on unbelieving Jerusalem. The Roman legions came from the east and the final destruction of Jerusalem was very swift. Their emblem was the eagle, and the carcass they came to feed on was Jerusalem.

The Sign of the Son of Man

> *Immediately after the tribulation of those days the sun will be darkened, and the moon will not give its light; the stars will fall from heaven, and the powers of the heavens will be shaken. Then the sign of the Son of Man will appear in heaven, and then all the tribes of the earth will mourn, and they will see the Son of Man coming on the clouds of heaven with*

power and great glory. And He will send His angels with a great sound
of a trumpet, and they will gather together His elect from the four winds,
from one end of heaven to the other. (Matthew 24:29-31)

In verse 3, the disciples asked Jesus what would be the *sign* of His coming. Jesus answers that question here. It would be immediately after the tribulation, the one described in verses 15-28, which was the destruction of Jerusalem and the Temple.

What is the sign? Jesus answers in a very apocalyptic style: After the destruction of the Jerusalem, the sun and moon would be darkened, the stars would fall and the heavens would be shaken. This is figurative language, following the prophetic idiom of the Old Testament, where the sun, moon and stars represented governing authorities.

Remember in Genesis 1, how the sun was to "rule" by day and the moon by night. Remember also Joseph's dream in Genesis 37 where the sun, moon and stars depicted his father, mother and eleven brothers all bowing down to him. We can also see it in Revelation 12:1, the great sign that appeared in heaven, where the woman is clothed with the sun, with the moon under her feet and a garland of twelve stars on her head, signifying her authority.

There are also prophecies of sun, moon and stars being darkened because of the judgments that would come upon Babylon (Isaiah 13:10), Edom (Isaiah 34:4-5) and Egypt (Ezekiel 32:7-8). These prophecies were fulfilled and all three nations were judged, even though the sun, moon and stars did not literally cease to shine.

The destruction of Jerusalem and the Temple was a sign that showed that they no longer had any authority. It was like the sun and moon going dark and the stars falling from the sky. The Temple system was done. Its destruction signified the end of that age and was the sign that the Son of Man was now ruling and reigning in heaven, for it was *His* judgment on Jerusalem that was being displayed.

Who were the "tribes of the earth" that mourned? These were the tribes of Israel. The Greek word for "earth" is *ge* and is often translated as "land." What land would that be? The land of which Jerusalem was a part, Israel. All the tribes of Israel mourned because they had just seen the judgment of God visited upon Jerusalem, just as Jesus had prophesied a generation earlier.

The language of the Son of Man "coming on the clouds of heaven with power and great glory," like the language of sun, moon and stars going dark and the heavens being shaken, is figurative. It signifies the triumph of His judgment. What He decreed in heaven would now be coming to pass on earth.

The gathering of the elect refers to the work of evangelizing the world, preaching the gospel and making disciples of all nations. The sound of a trumpet speaks of great proclamation. The word for "angels" literally means "messengers," and can refer to human messengers as well as heavenly ones. See, for example, Matthew 11:10, Mark 1:2, Luke 7:24, 27, and Luke 9:52. In each case, the word is *angellos*, but refers to human messengers.

The Parable of the Fig Tree

Now learn this parable from the fig tree: When its branch has already become tender and puts forth leaves, you know that summer is near. So you also, when you see all these things, know that it is near—at the doors! Assuredly, I say to you, this generation will by no means pass away till all these things take place. Heaven and earth will pass away, but My words will by no means pass away. (Matthew 24:32-35)

Here is where Jesus gives the time-stamp for when these things would occur. Jesus calls it a parable, which speaks of one thing in terms of another. Just as when a fig tree puts forth leaves, one can know that summer is near, likewise, when "you" (the disciples) see all these things, know that it is near. Then He uses a solemn formula, "Assuredly, I say to you," to emphasize what He is about to say next: "This generation will by no means pass away till all these things take place."

What are "all these things"? All the things He has spoken about in Matthew 24. Who does "this generation" mean? The Greek word for "generation" generally refers to one's contemporaries. Whose contemporaries is He talking about? Jesus says "this" generation, that is, the present one, not "that" generation, as if referring to some future one. Every time He speaks of a generation in the New Testament, He is referring to the one at hand, His contemporaries. Go back through this discourse and notice who He is addressing:

- Take heed that no one deceives *you* (v. 4).
- And *you* will hear of wars and rumors of war (v. 6).
- See that *you* are not troubled (v. 6).
- Then they will deliver *you* up to tribulation and kill *you*, and *you* will be hated by all nations for My sake (v. 9).
- When *you* see the abomination of desolation (v. 15).
- Pray that *your* flight may not be in winter (v. 20).
- Then if anyone says to *you* (v. 23).
- Therefore if they say to *you* (v. 26).
- Assuredly, I say to *you* (v. 33)
- So *you* also, when *you* see all these things, know that it is near (v. 33).

He is speaking to the disciples, and the generation He refers to in verse 34 is their own. They are of that generation which would not pass away until the events of this prophecy took place. The assurance that these things would happen within their time was His pronouncement: "Heaven and earth will pass away, but My words will by no means pass away." There is a strong claim to divinity inherent in this, for He speaks of *His* words in the same way He spoke of the Law in Matthew 5:18.

Everything Jesus discussed here—the abomination of desolation, great tribulation, the coming of the Son of Man on the clouds in judgment —was all fulfilled in the destruction of Jerusalem. And it all happened within a generation of when Jesus prophesied it.

An Hour You Do Not Expect

But of that day and hour no one knows, not even the angels of heaven, but My Father only. But as the days of Noah were, so also will the coming of the Son of Man be. For as in the days before the flood, they were eating and drinking, marrying and giving in marriage, until the day that Noah entered the ark, and did not know until the flood came and took them all away, so also will the coming of the Son of Man be. (Matthew 24:36-39)

Though Jesus revealed the generation in which all these things would happen, He did not give them the day and the hour. It was not His to tell—only the Father knew. It would be like the days of Noah, when the wicked carried on with life as usual until judgment came upon them. In the same way, Jerusalem would be carrying on with life as usual until the Son of Man came in judgment on her.

However, the certainty of this coming destruction did not mean that none would survive: "Then two men will be in the field: one will be taken and the other left. Two women will be grinding at the mill: one will be taken and the other left" (vv. 40-41). Some would be destroyed or carried off, others would remain. The prudent thing, then, would be to stay alert and prepared:

Be watchful, therefore, for you do not know what hour your Lord is coming. But know this, that if the master of the house had known what hour the thief would come, he would have watched and not allowed his house to be broken into. Therefore you also be ready, for the Son of Man is coming at an hour you do not expect. (Matthew 24:42-44)

Just as watchfulness was crucial when King Jesus brought judgment on unbelieving Israel at the end of the Temple age, so will it be when Jesus comes at the end of this present age.

THE KINGDOM OF THE WISE

When the gospel of the kingdom has been preached in all the world, the end of *this* age will come and Jesus will finally appear in all His glory. How do we prepare ourselves for this so that it does not take us by surprise?

> *Who then is a faithful and wise servant, whom his master made ruler over his household, to give them food in due season? Blessed is that servant whom his master, when he comes, will find so doing. Assuredly, I say to you that he will make him ruler over all his goods. But if that evil servant says in his heart, "My master is delaying his coming," and begins to beat his fellow servants, and to eat and drink with the drunkards, the master of that servant will come on a day when he is not looking for him and at an hour that he is not aware of, and will cut him in two and appoint him his portion with the hypocrites. There shall be weeping and gnashing of teeth. (Matthew 24:45-51)*

We do not know the hour of our Lord's return, but the best way to prepare for it is to fulfill what He has given us to do and treat properly those He has placed in front of us. This is wisdom, for He will always reward faithfulness but will deal severely with faithlessness and hypocrisy.

> *Then the kingdom of heaven shall be likened to ten virgins who took their lamps and went out to meet the bridegroom. Now five of them were wise, and five were foolish. Those who were foolish took their lamps and took no oil with them, but the wise took oil in their vessels with their lamps. But while the bridegroom was delayed, they all slumbered and slept. And at midnight a cry was heard: "Behold, the bridegroom is coming; go out to meet him!" Then all those virgins arose and trimmed their lamps. And the foolish said to the wise, "Give us some of your oil, for our lamps are going out." But the wise answered, saying, "No, lest there should not be enough for us and you; but go rather to those who sell, and buy for*

yourselves." And while they went to buy, the bridegroom came, and those who were ready went in with him to the wedding; and the door was shut. Afterward the other virgins came also, saying, "Lord, Lord, open to us!" But he answered and said, "Assuredly, I say to you, I do not know you. Watch therefore, for you know neither the day nor the hour in which the Son of Man is coming." (Matthew 25:1-13)

Though we hope Jesus will come sooner, His return may well be later than we think. It is easy to keep watch for a short while but it requires persevering faith to remain watchful and ready over an indefinite length of time. It is wisdom to be prepared, not only for the *return* of the Lord, but also for His *delay*.

The Kingdom of the Faithful

Well done, good and faithful servant; you have been faithful over a few things, I will make you ruler over many things. Enter into the joy of your Lord. (Matthew 25:21)

In the previous parables, Jesus cautions us to be ready for His return by watchfulness and faithfulness in our assignment. In this parable, we see another dimension of faithfulness: The increase of the kingdom of Heaven on Earth.

The kingdom of heaven is like a man traveling to a far country, who called his own servants and delivered his goods to them. And to one he gave five talents, to another two, and to another one, to each according to his own ability; and immediately he went on a journey. (Matthew 25:14-15)

Notice that each servant was given an amount "according to his own ability." Nobody was given what he could not handle, but whatever the amount given, the master expected it to be put to use and enlarged.

Then he who had received the five talents went and traded with them, and made another five talents. And likewise he who had received two gained two more also. But he who had received one went and dug in the ground, and hid his lord's money. (Matthew 25:16-18)

The first two servants put their talents to good use. When the master returned he found that they had both doubled his money. Perhaps they developed businesses which were very profitable. Or perhaps they simply invested their money at interest. Six to eight per cent was a common rate in those days and they would have easily been able to double their money in nine to twelve years. Maybe that is how long the master had been gone.

The third servant, however, simply buried his talent in the ground. He had the ability to do more and the opportunity to double his master's money just as the others did, but he did nothing.

After a long time the lord of those servants came and settled accounts with them. So he who had received five talents came and brought five other talents, saying, "Lord, you delivered to me five talents; look, I have gained five more talents besides them." His lord said to him, "Well done, good and faithful servant; you were faithful over a few things, I will make you ruler over many things. Enter into the joy of your lord."

He also who had received two talents came and said, "Lord, you delivered to me two talents; look, I have gained two more talents besides them." His lord said to him, "Well done, good and faithful servant; you have been faithful over a few things, I will make you ruler over many things. Enter into the joy of your lord." (Matthew 25:19-23)

The issue here is faithfulness. Each servant had been given funds to manage according to his ability, so competency was not a problem. All were competent, but not all were faithful. The Greek word for "faithful" is *pistos*, which is the same word for "faith." Today we often think of faithfulness as loyalty and trustworthiness. But at its core, there is a very important element of faith. These first two servants were faithful because they had faith in their master, his words and his purpose. They were trustworthy because they trusted. They knew how to trust *him* in a few things, so the master knew he could trust *them* with many things. They were faithful.

> *Then he who had received the one talent came and said, "Lord, I knew you to be a hard man, reaping where you have not sown, and gathering where you have not scattered seed. And I was afraid, and went and hid your talent in the ground. Look, there you have what is yours."*
>
> *But his lord answered and said to him, "You wicked and lazy servant, you knew that I reap where I have not sown, and gather where I have not scattered seed. So you ought to have deposited my money with the bankers, and at my coming I would have received back my own with interest. Therefore take the talent from him, and give it to him who has ten talents. For to everyone who has, more will be given, and he will have abundance; but from him who does not have, even what he has will be taken away. And cast the unprofitable servant into the outer darkness. There will be weeping and gnashing of teeth." (Matthew 25:24-30)*

The problem with the third servant is that he did not trust his master. He saw him as hard, stingy and oppressive, someone who exploited the labor of others. Because he had no faith, he was full of fear: "I was afraid, and went and hid your talent in the ground." It is reminiscent of the answer Adam gave after he sinned, and God asked him, "Where are you?" Adam said, "I was afraid ... and I hid" (Genesis 3:9-10).

The servant did not really know his master, but the master had him pretty well pegged—wicked and lazy! The master took on his servant's argument, though he did not agree with it. "So if you thought I was oppressive, and an exploiter"—that was the sense of his words—"then you should have put my money with the bankers so that I would at least have a little return on my investment." Taking the money to the Exchange would have required little more effort than to bury it in the ground. It would have been just as safe, if not safer, and would have gathered interest—sweat free. How lazy does a person have to be to pass that one up? But the servant not only lacked faith, he was paralyzed with fear. He could not look past his own security and see the larger picture, the increase of his master's interests.

Now consider the consequences. The first two servants, because they were faithful in little things, were made rulers over great things, while the fearful servant lost even the one talent he had; it was given to the one who now had ten talents. Faithful diligence brings abundance but those who are lazy and fearful will lose all they have.

The kingdom of Heaven on Earth is all about the rule and reign of God. He is looking for those who will trust Him completely and obey Him diligently, even in little things. He desires to enlarge His kingdom through us and make us rulers over great things. The reward is great, both now and forever.

THOSE WHO INHERIT THE KINGDOM

When the Son of Man comes in his glory, and all the angels with him, he will sit on his throne in heavenly glory. All the nations will be gathered before him, and he will separate the people one from another as a shepherd separates the sheep from the goats. He will put the sheep on his right and the goats on his left.

Then the King will say to those on his right, "Come, you who are blessed by my Father; take your inheritance, the kingdom prepared for you since the creation of the world. For I was hungry and you gave me something to eat, I was thirsty and you gave me something to drink, I was a stranger and you invited me in, I needed clothes and you clothed me, I was sick and you looked after me, I was in prison and you came to visit me."

Then the righteous will answer him, "Lord, when did we see you hungry and feed you, or thirsty and give you something to drink? When did we see you a stranger and invite you in, or needing clothes and clothe you? When did we see you sick or in prison and go to visit you?"

The King will reply, "I tell you the truth, whatever you did for one of the least of these brothers of mine, you did for me."

Then he will say to those on his left, "Depart from me, you who are cursed, into the eternal fire prepared for the devil and his angels. For I was hungry and you gave me nothing to eat, I was thirsty and you gave me nothing to drink, I was a stranger and you did not invite me in, I needed clothes and you did not clothe me, I was sick and in prison and you did not look after me."

They also will answer, "Lord, when did we see you hungry or thirsty or a stranger or needing clothes or sick or in prison, and did not help you?"

He will reply, "I tell you the truth, whatever you did not do for one of the least of these, you did not do for me."

Then they will go away to eternal punishment, but the righteous to eternal life. (Matthew 25:31-46)

There are two groups: the sheep and the goats. These are the nations of the world, not just the governmental entities, but all the people. In Bible times, sheep were highly valued while goats were considered something of a nuisance and required different handling.

Jesus is the Son of Man, the King who separates the nations as a shepherd separates the sheep from the goats. The sheep are lined up at His right hand, the hand of favor. The goats are placed at His left hand, signifying dishonor.

What is the basis for this separation? Here is where many people misinterpret this parable. They think that it is based on how the poor and needy in general are treated. That is, those who remember the poor and needy, and treat them well, are the sheep; those who neglect them are the goats.

Certainly we should always be mindful of the poor and needy to be hospitable toward them and show them kindness. God has always displayed His heart for the poor, and every good Jew in Jesus' day would have understood that it was part of his moral duty to look after them properly. The same is required of Christians today.

That, however, is not what Jesus is talking about in this parable. He is not referring to the hungry, the thirsty, the stranger, the naked, the sick and the imprisoned in general. He is speaking about a particular group: "these My brethren." Earlier in Matthew, Jesus clearly identified those who are His brothers.

> *While Jesus was still talking to the crowd, his mother and brothers stood out-side, wanting to speak to him. Someone told him, "Your mother and brothers are standing outside, wanting to speak to you." He replied to him, "Who is my mother, and who are my brothers?" Pointing to his disciples, he said, "Here are my mother and my brothers. For whoever does the will of my Father in heaven is my brother and sister and mother." (Matthew 12:46-50)*

Who are His brothers? Those who do the will of His Father. When asked, "What shall we do, that we may work the works of God," Jesus answered, "This is the work of God, that you believe in Him whom He sent" (John 6:28-29). His disciples—all who confess Jesus Christ as Savior and King—are His brothers. To receive them is to receive Him; to reject them is to reject Him.

> *He who receives you receives me, and he who receives me receives the one who sent me. Anyone who receives a prophet because he is a prophet will receive a prophet's reward, and anyone who receives a righteous man because he is a righteous man will receive a righteous man's reward. And if anyone gives even a cup of cold water to one of these little ones because he is my disciple, I tell you the truth, he will certainly not lose his reward. (Matthew 10:40-42)*

To receive the disciples of Jesus is to receive the message they bring—the gospel of Christ—and thus receive the Lord Jesus Himself. How we respond is the difference between eternal life and everlasting punishment.

The whole world is divided into two groups: those who receive the gospel of Christ and those who reject it. Those who receive it are blessed. They inherit the kingdom prepared for them from the foundation of the world—the kingdom of Heaven on Earth.

The Victorious Kingdom

The sobering events Jesus described in Matthew 24, which would happen within a generation, and the accompanying teaching in Matthew 25, on how to be prepared for His coming, must have left the disciples wide-eyed. But what was about to happen next would stretch them beyond their breaking point. After Jesus spoke all those things, He said, almost matter-of-factly, "You know that after two days is the Passover, and the Son of Man will be delivered up to be crucified" (Matthew 26:2).

But wait! What about the kingdom? Was it all coming to an end when it was only now just beginning? How can this be? And how could such a terrible thing happen to the Messiah King? The disciples must have been very perplexed, if not in denial. And yet, it was true. Even now the chief priests and Jewish leaders, who had been so offended, even outraged, at Jesus' ministry, were conspiring before Caiaphas, the high priest, "to take Jesus by trickery and kill Him" (v. 4).

When Jesus was in Bethany, at the house of Simon the leper, a woman came with an alabaster jar of very expensive and fragrant oil. Breaking it open, she emptied it all out over His head. Though she may not have realized it, this lavish act carried a prophetic significance. Jesus said, "For in pouring this fragrant oil on My body, she did it for My burial" (v. 12). Then Judas Iscariot, who was indignant at the waste of such expensive oil (John 12:4-5), went out and betrayed Jesus to the conspiracy (v. 14-16).

The Table of the Kingdom

But I say to you, I will not drink of this fruit of the vine from now on until that day when I drink it new with you in My Father's kingdom. (Matthew 26:29)

The preparations were all made and the Passover was now here. The disciples gathered to celebrate the meal with Jesus. As they were eating, Jesus announced that one of them would betray Him. They each began questioning, "Lord, is it I?" None of them suspected any of the others. They each realized what they themselves were capable of doing. However, though each had experienced moments of unbelief and denial, none had crossed over the line into the deep betrayal about which Jesus now spoke, except one: "The Son of Man indeed goes just as it is written of Him, but woe to that man by whom the Son of Man is betrayed! It would have been good for that man if he had not been born" (v. 24).

Then Judas, even in the midst of betraying Him, asked, "Rabbi, is it I?" Jesus answered, "You have said it" (v. 25). John records that Judas immediately went out after that (John 13:26-30).

As the others continued to eat and celebrate, Jesus took up symbols of the Passover meal and gave them new meaning:

> *And as they were eating, Jesus took bread, blessed and broke it, and gave it to the disciples and said, "Take, eat; this is My body."*
> *Then He took the cup, and gave thanks, and gave it to them, saying, "Drink from it, all of you. For this is My blood of the new covenant, which is shed for many for the remission of sins." (vv. 26-28)*

With these words, He instituted a new meal that would continue to be celebrated far beyond that night, the Table of the Lord. It is a divine sign that speaks of the giving of His body and the shedding of His blood—His death for our sake. It speaks of the new covenant we have now with God through Him, a better covenant established on better promises (Hebrews 8:6). But it also speaks of a richer fulfillment when Jesus returns.

With fervent desire I have desired to eat this Passover with you before I suffer; for I say to you, I will no longer eat of it until it is fulfilled in the kingdom of God ... Take this and divide it among yourselves; for I say to you, I will not drink of the fruit of the vine until the kingdom of God comes. (Luke 22:15-18)

The Table of the Lord speaks of the fulfillment of the kingdom of God. Jesus came announcing that it was already "at hand." Indeed, He spoke of it as being present within His disciples (Luke 17:21). However, it is not yet fulfilled. It has not yet come in all its completeness. That will not happen until the King Himself returns.

In Matthew's reading, the word "new," does not refer to newness of time but to newness of quality. Jesus will drink this wine with us in the completeness of His kingdom. The Table of the Lord, then, is a sign that the King of Heaven and Earth will return. Paul reminds us, "For as often as you eat this bread and drink this cup, you proclaim the Lord's death *till He comes*" (1 Corinthians 11:26).

Not only is this Table a sign of the Father's kingdom, it also shows that we are participants in that kingdom, that we truly belong to it, for the Lord promises that He will drink of this wine *with* us. We participate in His kingdom not merely as servants but as sons. John said, "As many as received Him, to them He gave the right to become children of God, to those who believe in His name" (John 1:12). Through faith in King Jesus the Messiah, we become the sons of God, and as sons, heirs of His kingdom. Jesus said, "It is your Father's good pleasure to give you the kingdom" (Luke 12:32). The fullness of this kingdom is our inheritance, our birthright.

The Table of the Lord is the sign that, though the kingdom of Heaven on Earth is already present and active within us, we shall one day experience it in all its glory when Jesus returns.

The Passion and Resurrection of the King

All this was done that the Scriptures of the prophets might be fulfilled.
(Matthew 26:56)

After the Passover meal, they sang the traditional hymn, the last part of the *Hallel* cycle (Psalms 114-118) and went out to the Mount of Olives (v. 30). Jesus said,

> *All of you will be made to stumble because of Me this night, for it is written:*
> *"I will strike the Shepherd. And the sheep of the flock will be scattered."*
> *But after I have been raised, I will go before you to Galilee. (vv. 31-32)*

He was quoting one of the prophets, Zechariah 13:7, which spoke of a time of severe testing. Peter declared that he would never be made to stumble because of Jesus. The Lord said to him, "Assuredly, I say to you that this night, before the rooster crows, you will deny Me three times," but still Peter insisted (vv. 33-35).

Jesus went to the garden of Gethsemane, taking Peter, James and John with Him. They did not realize it then but this was the last hour they would be with Him before He was taken. They were very sleepy. He went off a little ways and began to pray: "O My Father, if it is possible, let this cup pass from Me; nevertheless, not as I will but as You will" (v. 39). When He came back, He had to wake them. He went off and prayed a second time, "O my Father, if this cup cannot pass away from Me unless I drink, Your will be done" (v. 42). He came back again, and again had to wake them. He went and prayed the same prayer for a third time. When He returned, He once again had to wake the disciples:

> *Are you still sleeping and resting? Behold, the hour is at hand, and the Son*
> *of Man is being betrayed into the hands of sinners. Rise, let us be going.*
> *See, My betrayer is at hand. (vv. 45-46).*

Judas now approached, along with the chief priests and elders. He identified Jesus to them with a kiss. One of the disciples (John 18:10 identifies him as Peter) drew his sword and cut off the ear of Malchus, the servant of the high priest. Jesus said to Peter:

> *Put your sword in its place, for all who take the sword will perish by the sword. Or do you think that I cannot now pray to My Father, and He will provide Me with more than twelve legions of angels? How then could the Scriptures be fulfilled, that it must happen thus? (vv. 52-54)*

Then turning to the mob, He said:

> *Have you come out, as against a robber, with swords and clubs to take Me? I sat daily with you, teaching in the temple, and you did not seize Me. But all this was done that the Scriptures of the prophets might be fulfilled. (vv. 55-56)*

That the Scriptures Might Be Fulfilled

What was now happening had been foretold in the Scriptures. Jesus knew ahead of time where His ministry would lead: To the Cross. He could have chosen otherwise—that was the agony of Gethsemane—but "how then could the Scriptures be fulfilled?" Indeed, "all this was done that the Scriptures of the prophets might be fulfilled." Foremost among the passages that come to mind is the *Song of the Suffering Servant* in Isaiah 52:13-53:12. It is a messianic prophecy:

> *Behold, My Servant shall deal prudently;*
> *   He shall be exalted and extolled and be very high.*
> *Just as many were astonished at you,*
> *   So His visage was marred more than any man,*
> *   And His form more than the sons of men;*
> *So shall He sprinkle many nations.*

Kings shall shut their mouths at Him;
For what had not been told them they shall see,
    And what they had not heard they shall consider.

Who has believed our report?
    And to whom has the arm of the LORD *been revealed?*
For He shall grow up before Him as a tender plant,
    And as a root out of dry ground.
He has no form or comeliness;
    And when we see Him,
    There is no beauty that we should desire Him.
He is despised and rejected by men,
    A Man of sorrows and acquainted with grief.
And we hid, as it were, our faces from Him;
    He was despised, and we did not esteem Him.

Surely He has borne our griefs
    And carried our sorrows;
Yet we esteemed Him stricken,
    Smitten by God, and afflicted.
But He was wounded for our transgressions,
    He was bruised for our iniquities;
The chastisement for our peace was upon Him,
    And by His stripes we are healed.
All we like sheep have gone astray;
    We have turned, every one, to his own way;
    And the LORD *has laid on Him the iniquity of us all.*

He was oppressed and He was afflicted,
    Yet He opened not His mouth;
He was led as a lamb to the slaughter,
    And as a sheep before its shearers is silent,
    So He opened not His mouth.

He was taken from prison and from judgment,
And who will declare His generation?
For He was cut off from the land of the living;
For the transgressions of My people He was stricken.
And they made His grave with the wicked—
But with the rich at His death,
Because He had done no violence,
Nor was any deceit in His mouth.

Yet it pleased the LORD to bruise Him;
He has put Him to grief.
When You make His soul an offering for sin,
He shall see His seed, He shall prolong His days,
And the pleasure of the LORD shall prosper in His hand.
He shall see the labor of His soul, and be satisfied.
By His knowledge My righteous Servant shall justify many,
For He shall bear their iniquities.
Therefore I will divide Him a portion with the great,
And He shall divide the spoil with the strong,
Because He poured out His soul unto death,
And He was numbered with the transgressors,
And He bore the sin of many,
And made intercession for the transgressors.

For our sake and the sake of Heaven on Earth, it was necessary for this Scripture to be fulfilled. The kingdom of God is a kingdom of righteousness, therefore our iniquity must be fully dealt with. Everything Jesus suffered was for our benefit: He was despised and rejected on our behalf (v. 3). He bore our griefs and sorrows (v.4). He was wounded for our transgression, bruised for our iniquities (v. 5). He was chastised for the sake of our peace (v. 5). Without all this, Heaven on Earth could not be, for no one would be able to enter it.

Silent Before His Accusers

Like a lamb led to slaughter, Jesus was brought before the Jewish Sanhedrin. He did not resist. Like a sheep brought before the shearers, He did not defend Himself. False testimony was brought against Him, but He did not say anything. The high priest said, "Do You answer nothing? What is it these men testify against You?" But Jesus remained silent. The high priest said, "I put You under oath by the living God: Tell us if You are the Christ, the Son of God!" (Matthew 26:62).

Jesus answered, "It is as you said. Nevertheless, I say to you, hereafter you will see the Son of Man sitting at the right hand of the Power, and coming on the clouds of heaven" (v. 64). This spoke of His deity and His coming in judgment. It so infuriated the high priest and the council that they judged Him a blasphemer, worthy of death.

Having no authority to execute Jesus, they brought Him before the Roman governor, Pontius Pilate (Matthew 27:1-2). Pilate asked Him, "Are You the King of the Jews." Jesus answered, "It is as you say" (v. 12). Pilate said, "Do You not hear how many things they testify against You?" But Jesus said nothing. Pilate was astonished.

Since it was Passover, Pilate had the option, as was customary, of releasing a prisoner to the people. He offered them the choice between Jesus and an insurrectionist and murderer named Barabbas. The chief priests and elders persuaded the people to call for Barabbas. "What then shall I do with Jesus who is called Christ?" Pilate asked. "Let Him be crucified," they said. "Why, what evil has He done?" said Pilate. They cried out even louder, "Let Him be crucified." So Pilate handed Jesus over for scourging and crucifixion.

Death, Burial and Resurrection

A placard posting the charge was placed on the cross over Jesus' head: THIS IS JESUS THE KING OF THE JEWS. As He hung on the cross, darkness covered the land from noon until 3 p.m. Then Jesus "cried out with a loud voice, and yielded up His spirit" (v. 50). The veil of the Temple was split in two and the earth shook.

When evening came, Joseph, a rich man of Arimathea who was also a disciple of Jesus, took the body of Jesus, wrapped it in linen and laid it in a new cut tomb. A large stone was rolled into place, covering the opening. Mary Magdalene and another Mary were watching from nearby. The chief priests and Pharisees, remembering what Jesus said, "After three days, I will rise," had the Temple Guard go secure and watch the tomb.

On the third day, which was the first day of the week, the two Marys came to the tomb. There was an earthquake and an angel, and the stone was rolled away from the opening. The angel said to them, "Do not be afraid, for I know that you seek Jesus who was crucified. He is not here; for He is risen, as He said. Come, see the place where the Lord lay. And go quickly and tell His disciples that He is risen from the dead" (Matthew 28:5-7).

As they went, Jesus met them, saying, "Rejoice!" They came and worshipped at His feet. "Do not be afraid," He said, "Go and tell My brethren to go to Galilee, and there they will see Me" (vv. 9-10).

The eleven disciples—minus Judas, who had hanged himself, but including Peter who had denied Jesus three times—went to Galilee, to the mountain where Jesus told them to meet Him. When they saw Him, they worshipped Him.

ALL AUTHORITY IN HEAVEN AND EARTH

All authority has been given to Me in heaven and on earth. Go therefore and make disciples of all the nations, baptizing them in the name of the Father and of the Son and of the Holy Spirit, teaching them to observe all things that I have commanded you; and lo, I am with you always, even to the end of the age. Amen. (Matthew 28:18-20)

Jesus announced His victory to the disciples: "All authority has been given to Me in heaven and on earth." The full range of His dominion was now established, in His humanity as well as in His divinity, on earth as well as in heaven. This is as Daniel prophesied:

> *I was watching in the night visions,*
> *And behold, One like the Son of Man,*
> *Coming with the clouds of heaven!*
> *He came to the Ancient of Days,*
> *And they brought Him near before Him.*
> *Then to Him was given dominion and glory and a kingdom,*
> *That all peoples, nations, and languages should serve Him.*
> *His dominion is an everlasting dominion,*
> *Which shall not pass away,*
> *And His kingdom the one*
> *Which shall not be destroyed.*
>
> *(Daniel 7:13-14)*

All the dominion, power and the glory of the kingdom of Heaven on Earth has been given to Jesus, now and forever. With this authority, He gave the disciples their mission, which is called the Great Commission:

- *Go therefore and make disciples of all nations.* All nations belong under the authority of Heaven on Earth, therefore, all nations must be instructed in following Jesus the King.
- *Baptizing them in the name of the Father and of the Son and of the Holy Spirit.* Baptism is the sign that one has been initiated into faith in Jesus Christ.
- *Teaching them to observe all things that I have commanded you.* Everything Jesus taught and commanded the disciples, the disciples would now go and teach all nations. In this way, each new generation of disciples would teach the next.

This mission is backed with all the authority of heaven and earth, and Jesus has given us the promise of His presence: "I am with you always, even to the end of the age."

Matthew summarizes this for us, but Jesus also said other things at this time, which the other Gospel writers pick up on. The Gospel of Mark emphasizes the Great Commission this way:

> *And He said to them, "Go into all the world and preach the gospel to every creature. He who believes and is baptized will be saved; but he who does not believe will be condemned. And these signs will follow those who believe: In My name they will cast out demons; they will speak with new tongues; they will take up serpents; and if they drink anything deadly, it will by no means hurt them; they will lay hands on the sick, and they will recover."*
>
> *So then, after the Lord had spoken to them, He was received up into heaven, and sat down at the right hand of God. And they went out and preached everywhere, the Lord working with them and confirming the word through the accompanying signs. Amen. (Mark 16:15-20)*

Luke presents it this way in his Gospel and in the book of Acts:

> *Thus it is written, and thus it was necessary for the Christ to suffer and to rise from the dead the third day, and that repentance and remission of sins should be preached in His name to all nations, beginning at Jerusalem. And you are witnesses of these things. Behold, I send the Promise of My Father upon you; but tarry in the city of Jerusalem until you are endued with power from on high. (Luke 24:46-49)*

> *But you shall receive power when the Holy Spirit has come upon you; and you shall be witnesses to Me in Jerusalem, and in all Judea and Samaria, and to the end of the earth. (Acts 1:8)*

The rest of the book of Acts gives a more thorough narrative of the early stages of the Church as it began to accomplish this mission. As in Mark's brief version, the message of the gospel was often accompanied by signs, wonders and miracles of healing and exorcism—all in the power of the Holy Spirit. These and similar signs have continued to this day, revealing the kingdom of Heaven on Earth.*

Jesus said He would build His Church, and the gates of hell, the counsels and powers of the enemy, will not prevail against it (Matthew 16:18).

- He has given us the keys of the kingdom to bind on earth what has been bound in heaven and loose on earth what has been loosed in heaven (Matthew 16:19; Matthew 18:18).
- He has given us authority to pray for the kingdom of God to keep coming and the will of God to keep being done on earth as it is in heaven (Matthew 6:10).
- He has commissioned us with all the authority of heaven and earth behind us and the assurance that He is always with us (Matthew 28:18-20).
- He has given us the Holy Spirit and the power to preach the Gospel everywhere and bring the evidence of who He is into all the world (Acts 1:8).

His Church will prevail and its mission will succeed. All nations will be discipled and the kingdom of Heaven on Earth will continue to increase until King Jesus comes again.

---

*For a multitude of examples, see Jeff Doles, *Miracles and Manifestations of the Holy Spirit in the History of the Church* (Walking Barefoot Ministries, 2008).

BOOKS BY JEFF DOLES

*Miracles and Manifestations of the Holy Spirit
in the History of the Church*

*From the Manger to the Cross:
Advent and Christmas Meditations*

*God's Word in Your Mouth:
Changing Your World Through Faith*

*Praying with Fire:
Change Your World with the Powerful Prayers of the Apostles*

*Healing Scriptures and Prayers
(also available in CD and MP3)*

*The Faith Log:
Exploring the Dynamics of Biblical Faith*

*Walking Barefoot:
Living in Prayer, Faith and the Power of God*

Walking Barefoot Ministries
P. O. Box 1062
Seffner, FL 33583
www.walkingbarefoot.com

Also available at *Amazon.com*.

Also by Jeff Doles

Miracles and Manifestations of the Holy Spirit in the History of the Church

ISBN 978-0-09744748-9-2
9.6x7.4 in., 274 pages

Available at www.walkingbarefoot.com and Amazon.com.

Also by Jeff Doles

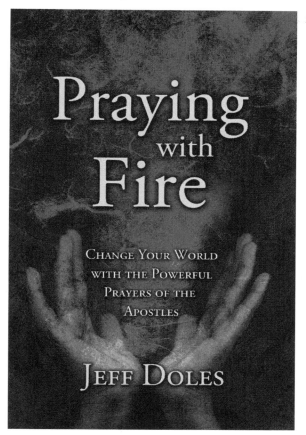

Praying With Fire
Change Your World with the
Powerful Prayers of the Apostles

ISBN 978-0-9744748-6-1
6x9 in., 104 pages

Available at www.walkingbarefoot.com and Amazon.com.

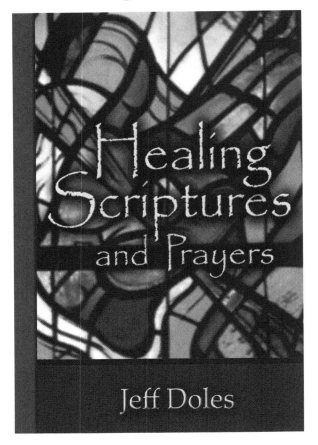

Healing Scriptures and Prayers

ISBN 978-0-9744748-1-6 (Paperback)
6 x 9 in. 120 pages

Available at www.walkingbarefoot.com and Amazon.com.

Soak in the Healing Scriptures

Vol. 1: Old Testament
Scriptures

Vol. 2: New Testament
Scriptures

Vol. 3: Healing
Names of God

Vol. 4: The Healing
Ministry of Jesus

Healing Scriptures and Prayers
In CD and MP3

Available at www.walkingbarefoot.com and Amazon.com.